FIGHTING ISIS

TIM LOCKS

PAN BOOKS

First published 2016 by Sidgwick & Jackson

First published in paperback 2017 by Pan Books
20 New Wharf Road, London N1 9RR
Associated companies throughout the world
www.panmacmillan.com

ISBN 978-1-5098-2443-4

1 3 5 7 9 8 6 4 2

A CIP catalogue record for this book is available from the British Library.

Typeset by Ellipsis Digital Limited, Glasgow
Printed and bound by CPI Group (UK) Ltd, Croydon, CR0 4YY

This book is sold subject to the condition that it shall not, by way of
tra   hout
the   than
tha   ding

To the man who has been my friend and mentor through thick and thin, who showed me never to be afraid of anything. You taught me not everyone can be educated, that some things in life can't be beaten and to never go downstairs empty-handed.
This is for you, mate.

CONTENTS

PROLOGUE

I studied the village of Batnaya, three kilometres away across the huge open expanse of flat, dusty, barren land. Squinting, I could make out signs of movement around the water tower, the whole scene shimmering in the afternoon heat.

Resting my elbows on the edge of the roof, I raised the scope and zoomed in until I was able to pick out some tiny figures. All the men were kitted out in black and carrying a black flag between them. Daesh.

This was my first day on the front line in Iraq. Finally, after battling months of frustrating red tape, I was here, and the enemy I had come to tackle was within sight.

'You know the General has already lost three of his brothers to Daesh?' asked Marcus, a local Assyrian from Dwekh Nawsha, the Christian militia group I was affiliated with. 'One of them was killed by a mortar round in the trench just down there, along with three of his men.'

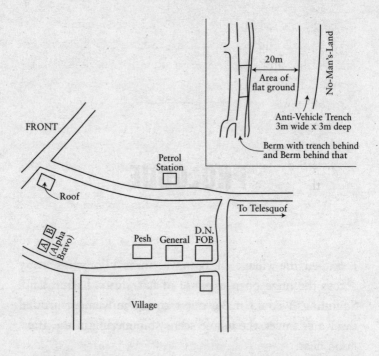

He gestured to the trench that lay in front of us. It had a berm behind it and in front of it, and twenty metres nearer to no-man's-land, which divided us from Daesh territory, was the anti-vehicle ditch, three metres wide and deep, dug during the fighting with Daesh. 'No question that the mortars could reach this far then,' I thought. There was a road that wound between Batnaya and our village, Baqofa, the only sign that life hadn't always been this way. No longer used, it was starting to disappear beneath the swirling dust.

Pushing off the wall, I headed back across the roof of our house to join JP, a fellow Brit, who was my closest friend in the group. The house had been abandoned by fleeing locals and was now being used to coordinate front-line action and offer support to any activities on the ground. It was being manned by the Peshmerga – the Kurdish army – with the help of Dwekh Nawsha.

'I've just been told that when we fire mortars at them, the aim is ultimately the water tower,' JP told me. 'But anywhere in the village is fine, just not the church. We avoid the church at all costs.'

He shrugged as he spoke, knowing we would both be thinking the same about that instruction. Neither of us was here for religious reasons, but rather because we wanted to help stop the slaughter of innocent people and destroy Daesh. But if that was their rule, we could live with it.

I had just pulled my phone out and begun taking photos of the area when suddenly there was a thud, and a thick cloud of dust sprang up from the ground four hundred metres away. A mortar! Adrenalin and excitement kicked in, making me instantly alert. I turned my phone in the direction of the dust, determined to record the first mortar round of my life.

There was a whoosh, and a second thump – another mortar round had slammed into the ground closer to us, this time around three hundred metres away. We'd been told no action was expected until night-time, when temperatures were cooler and both sides preferred to be active, but it looked like things were about to get interesting. This was most probably because Daesh had seen that we (the volunteers from the West) were there. They

3

watched us as much as we watched them, and had better kit with which to do it.

Then a third round came rushing in and landed two hundred metres away. Immediately the atmosphere on the roof changed.

'Fuck, they are dialling in on us. Get off the roof!' shouted Cory, a former US Army Ranger. It seemed they were aiming for our building, and a spotter was helping adjust the angle of the weapon one click at a time to hone in on their target – us.

The Americans and several of the Peshmerga soldiers ran to the side of the roof and sprinted down the concrete stairs shaped against the building (as handrail or guard) to get away, clearly fearful that the next mortar would be on target.

I looked around and stopped for a few moments to consider the options. I was in Iraq as a volunteer fighter, so I had no army commander to tell me what to do. Every decision I made was to be my own, and with no previous military experience it was all about using common sense and keeping level-headed. I followed suit and ran down the stairs.

Once on the ground I paused to see some people had disappeared towards the berm, a long thin earthen hill running parallel to and about twenty metres back from the vehicle trenches. Soft ground is a good area to be during mortar fire, as a mortar will go into the ground and explode, not bounce around as it can do on concrete. I hadn't experienced this first-hand yet, but I had done my research. I did, after all, want to survive out here.

The Americans were over to my left along with Marcus, and some of the Peshmerga were to my right, but there was a big gap opposite the abandoned road. If this was a pre-emptive strike before Daesh came in vehicles, I was sure this would be their route. If I set up there, I could take out as many Daesh as possible when they appeared in view.

Just then another mortar exploded, sounding even closer to us than the last. Keeping low, to make myself as small a target as possible, I sprinted to my destination. At least I attempted to sprint – I had 40 kilogrammes of kit weighing me down, as I had come out prepared for any eventuality. I had my Osprey combat vest on – body armour that covered my chest – and my machete was tucked in behind my shotgun. My Glock 19 was in a high leg holster, and my shotgun was on my back in a holster I had fashioned myself from an old Camelbak. It was on my Osprey on my back, and I had twelve magazines of 7.62mm ammunition for my AK47, six magazines of 9mm for my Glock, a pouch of approximately twenty shells for my shotgun, my personal medical kit and my personal admin pouch. We had got ourselves all kitted up, working on the proviso that until we knew what it was like on the front line, it was better to be prepared for anything. Most kit stays in the FOB – you basically carry ammo, water and meds.

I dived into a nice depression, and lay flat on the soft ground, shoving the front grip of my AK into the dirt and setting up my equipment around me. I was desperate to see Daesh heads appear over the horizon.

Wiping sweat from my brow – the heat had reached 45 degrees by now – I turned my comms on and radioed through to JP, who I could see still standing on the roof behind me. He responded, and to my surprise was laughing his head off.

'Big T, you are the first civilian I have ever seen running *towards* mortar fire. I'm not sure if that makes you crazy or brave.'

'Why are you still on the roof?' I asked, laughing too with the adrenalin of it all.

'Tex has run to the mortar to man that. I'm going to direct him, and I can do that best from up here with the scope.'

JP is ex-army, pragmatic, fearless, and of the opinion that if it is your time to die, it is your time, and that is that. So the fact he had stayed on the roof, prioritizing his role over his own safety, made sense to me.

Just then, Dushka fire also started to ring out over my head. These are long-range 12.7mm machine guns; they are one of the weapons of choice of both sides, and make a hell of a noise. I flattened myself into the soil. They clearly meant business.

But despite the bullets flying overhead, I couldn't help a smile. This is what I had wanted for so long, what I had spent months planning for – to get to the front line and defend innocent people against the horrors of Daesh. Now, finally, it was happening.

1

I JOIN THE FIGHT

I have wanted to be a soldier for as long as I can remember. As a kid I was always the one wanting to play war games, and in my teens I had posters from the Gulf War on my walls. I would lie in bed imagining I was out fighting alongside these men, and think about the incredible bravery and strength each of them had. I'm not someone who spends a lot of time reading but I became obsessed with *Bravo Two Zero* by Andy McNab, reading it again and again, until I knew all the events off by heart. There was no question for me that all these members of the British forces were the ultimate good guys, taking on all the world's bad guys.

My parents were not so keen on my career plans, however. One day as a young boy I was told to give up anything of a 'paramilitary' nature from my room, which included my Gulf War posters, plastic toy guns and even my favourite baseball cap, just because it had a camouflage design.

My dad once arranged for me to go on an open day with the Parachute Regiment. I loved everything about my trip – the facilities, the fitness test, the gear . . . What teenage boy is not going to enjoy running around and climbing things for a day!

I started boarding school from seven, and was never happy there. I genuinely detested it, but my parents were determined I needed to remain.

Don't get me wrong, I realize they spent thousands of pounds on my education, and did it with the best of intentions to give me what they saw as the best start in life, for which I am grateful. A preparatory school followed by Stowe School in Buckinghamshire are places some people would give anything to attend. But it really wasn't for me. I have never been a natural conformist, and accepting authority without question is not something that sits well for me, at least not from teachers who gave me no reason to respect them. As a result I was constantly playing up and answering back, getting into trouble at every opportunity. I always felt it would have been different in the army as my seniors would have accomplished things that meant they earned respect, and I would have had no problem following their orders.

A school rule meant each student was allowed one magazine subscription. I immediately opted for *Combat and Survival*, but it wasn't long before my choice of reading got back to my family, and my short-lived subscription was cancelled.

But one of the biggest issues for me was the fact I was

quite badly bullied during my school years. Back then I was a skinny kid, without an ounce of muscle, and no fighting skills to speak of. I didn't have a set of friends to back me up, and with no home to escape to at night the endless taunts and finding my belongings constantly going missing was incredibly draining. Ever since my school days it has been hugely important to me to support the underdog, and help any victim of bullying, and I suppose that's because I know exactly how they are feeling.

If I took anything beneficial from boarding school, it was an ability to live in close proximity with a bunch of other guys, and a near-OCD level of tidiness and organization, all of which have stayed with me since, and in the last couple of years have proved very useful.

Stowe was to be my home until the sixth form, when, miserable and angry that I hadn't been allowed to leave school at sixteen, I repeatedly ran away. After a year, I had gone AWOL so many times that the school refused to take me back. Still not in the clear though, I was sent to college in London to do my A-levels, but hated it so much that although I sat the exams, I failed them. It was a waste of time and money, and I wish I had stuck to my guns and left school at sixteen as I had wanted.

After finally escaping from education, the challenge was to decide my next plan of action. I tried to join as a private but failed the 'learning test', so instead I got a job at Thorpe Park in Chertsey, Surrey, then moved into door security on local nightclubs, in particular one called Cheekies. I was still skinny and slight, but I quickly took to it, and worked my way up, becoming part of a seventeen-man team. The head doorman took me under his wing, training me up, and giving me his opinions on my life both on and off the door. He became like a father figure to me, and we are still very close today. At the same time I began going to the gym and bulking up, and found I loved it. Quickly the gym became part of my daily routine, to feel good about myself, but also as a kind of refuge. I would work out on a different body part each day. It became such a part of my life that even today if I don't get my daily gym hit, I feel a bit on edge.

After that I became a prison officer at HMP Feltham for four years, working first with eighteen- to twenty-one-year-olds who were on remand, and then with those who were in jail with mental-health problems. That was quite something, and I dealt with a fair few very troubled and violent people.

Then I started working in construction, and finally I figured I had had enough of working for other people and decided to start my own company. It was in this area I was most successful, building up a decent business for myself. I would start the day earlier than most people – I'd be up and out by 5 am because I wanted to be finished as early as possible and enjoy my life.

By the start of the summer of 2014 I had created a pretty good set-up for myself and put aside some good money that allowed me to make changes to my house – a swimming pool in the garden and an outdoor bar were my two favourites. At thirty-seven years old I had created the perfect bachelor pad! I was in good shape physically, I had a great social life, and although none of my serious relationships had lasted, I was happy with the way things were and life was in a good place. But as always seemed to happen with me, I was restless and ready to find a new adventure. I was considering moving to Bodrum in south-west Turkey for a while. I loved it out there, and had taken four holidays there the previous year alone. Being on the coast, the pace of life, and the friendly people all really appealed to me.

But as I was considering how to make the plan a reality, I was getting more and more disturbed by the international news I was seeing on the TV, in particular involving Daesh in the Middle East. They were a militant group that had been set up in 1999, but it wasn't until early 2014 that they started gaining news coverage, when they began making genuine inroads against the Iraqi army, taking Fallujah, Ramadi and then Mosul. Then in June 2014 they declared themselves a caliphate, claiming religious, political and military authority over Muslims worldwide, under the rule of Abu Bakr-al Baghdadi. What had seemed to be just the latest in a long line of wannabe terrorist organizations bothering the edge of society was actually gathering momentum to become a force that was causing real and tangible damage to the world, and showing very little regard for human life. Hundreds of thousands of people had been made homeless, others had been executed. Images on social media of Syrian soldiers being beheaded were the first indication of what was to become a regular method of punishment.

I began following groups on Facebook set up by people concerned about the incidents and giving insider info, and I shared the stories on my own wall to raise awareness. The world seemed to be becoming more dangerous; extremism was running rife with no one standing up to stop the atrocities.

In August things escalated, with Daesh expanding into the north of Iraq and taking control of lots of key cities in just two weeks. I watched as the news unfolded, with more cities listed each day. Zumar, Wana, Mosul Dam, Tel Keppe, Kocho, Bakhdida, Karamlish, Bartella, Makmour and Sinjar, one by one they came under the control of Daesh. The statistics were shocking. The minority community of three hundred thousand Iraqi and Yazidi Christians had been driven from their homes, in what was effectively ethnic cleansing.

The turning point for me was one sunny day when I got home from work and settled down to eat lunch in front of the television. The news was focused on Mount Sinjar in Iraq, where fifty thousand Yazidis had been forced to flee in desperation to escape Daesh.

I sat glued as the television footage showed them trapped on the mountain without food, water, shelter and life's basics. Another five thousand Yazidi men had been massacred in Sinjar, and around seven thousand Yazidi women taken as slaves. The full horror of their fate was only to become clearer later – sold into sex slavery, raped, killed if they tried to escape. I felt sickened and disgusted that the world had sat and watched the growing problem of Daesh, and allowed things to get this far. It was clear this was more than just your average fanatical group rearing its head and disappearing weeks later. The Middle East obviously had a serious problem and I felt the rest of the world needed to get involved. After a few days the Iraqi military began airdropping supplies to the refuges, later joined by the US, and finally the UK, but as far as I was concerned, it was not even a drop in the ocean of what should be done. This was temporary relief for those poor people on the mountain, not a long-term solution for them, or anyone else that Daesh would line up as their next target.

That night in the pub I began discussing it with a friend. As I blasted everyone from governments to militaries and even individuals for doing nothing about it, something suddenly clicked. Sure, I had voiced my disgust on Facebook, and shared stories, but what was I actually doing about it? Why was I going to piss about on a boat in Turkey for a few months, when I could actually do something useful by helping tackle the growing horror of Daesh?

'I am going to go over there and join the fight,' I told my friend. He laughed, then realized I might be serious.

'It's one of the worst things I have seen,' I continued. 'It is bullying on the worst kind of scale and you know I can't stand that. If I carried on just enjoying myself knowing what those people are going through, well then I'd be a hypocrite.'

The next day my friend called me. 'Tim, you know all that chat last night about you going out to take on Daesh, it was just the drink talking, right?'

But I had to tell him no, I was serious. When I get an idea in my head that I feel so strongly about, I am not a person to back away from it. This had become real for me.

Over the next few months I began sending messages to a few people from the Facebook sites I was following, in particular Jordan Matson, an American ex-soldier. He was one of the first Westerners to go out and fight against Daesh in Syria, as like me he had felt he could not sit at home and watch this mindless killing and destruction of the little peace that had been established in the Middle East.

He had joined YPG (it roughly translates into English as the People's Protection Units), a Kurdish-run armed service that was tackling Daesh in Syria. They often fought alongside the Syrian opposition fighters, but at the same time were avoiding becoming too involved in the internal battle for Syria, by avoiding conflict with the Syrian government. Their main aim was to secure Kurdish areas of the land against Daesh, and stop any atrocities against people in the area. While the majority of fighters were Kurdish, they were keen for anyone to join who supported the cause, and as such had various Assyrian Christian units, Arabs, Turks, and now Westerners beginning to swell the ranks. It sounded like the right kind of group for me to become involved with.

Within a month of arriving, Jordan had been hit by a mortar, and while recovering had set up a campaign called Lions of Rojava to encourage Western fighters to join him.

I also began chatting to another guy at YPG, an ex-US Marine called Josh, who was able to tell me a lot about the process of getting out there, and was keen to be as helpful as possible.

Josh advised me on getting equipment, warned me I would have to pay for everything myself and filled me in on some of the situation. He wanted to be sure I wasn't some deluded Brit with a romantic idea of war. Apparently a worrying number of the people in touch with him had an incredibly unrealistic idea of what fighting alongside YPG would be like.

One key thing that Josh taught me was to refer to Daesh as Daesh, and not IS (Islamic State), ISIS (Islamic State in Iraq and Syria), ISIL (Islamic State of Iraq and the Levant), or any of the other names that they wanted to be known as in their ongoing PR campaign. As he explained it: 'If you call them any of those acronyms, you are accepting that they are an Islamic State of sorts, and well, they aren't. It makes them seem legitimate, and that is the last thing they are. It is pretty ignorant of all the press and politicians who have fallen for their rhetoric, so make sure you don't do the same! Besides, everyone out here calls them Daesh, so it will help you fit in better with the locals.'

He explained that the name Daesh is a rough acronym for the Arabic for Islamic State in Iraq and the Levant – 'Al-Dawla al-Islamiya fi Iraq wa al-Sham' – but that Daesh hated the shortened version. There were various theories as to why, but they made it very clear that they did, cutting out the tongues and flogging anyone in areas they controlled that used the acronym. The fact they felt so strongly against it was all the motivation I needed to use it!

Daesh were proving to be very adept at PR-ing themselves on a global scale. It wasn't just about the name, but their online presence as well. They were able to get their message out through all sorts of websites and online videos, and their recruitment had gone into overdrive through social media. It wasn't just young Muslim men disillusioned with life who were encouraged to flee abroad to fight for them: stories had begun emerging about young non-Muslim females becoming infatuated with the ideals, and fighters they hadn't even met, and running off to Syria to become Daesh brides. So using a different name for them was a small step, but for a group for whom image was so crucial, anything that could help was worth trying.

It was now a few months on from the day I saw the Mount Sinjar news, and all my research had only served to strengthen my resolve. I felt motivated by the stories from those already out there fighting, but also by the news reports that revealed more horrific acts on a daily basis. Gay men blindfolded and thrown from the tops of buildings, women stoned to death on the word of sadistic old men, people stoned, mutilated and crucified in front of baying mobs. Every day I remained in the UK was a day I could be out there trying to stop this. It was time to prepare in earnest. I started winding down my business, began eBaying all my belongings and put my house up for sale. Perhaps I could have rented it out, but it seemed like extra hassle, and let's face it, I didn't know if I would be coming back and that would mean more hassle for someone else to sell or organize. I had tried not to focus on it too much, but I was realistic that death was a distinct possibility on the path I was choosing to take. I had reconciled myself with that, partly as I have never thought I would live to an old age anyway. I believe in living life to the maximum, and have always known that could mean dying young. But also, if I was to throw myself one hundred per cent behind this cause, then I had to see the bigger picture, and if the risk of my death was necessary to change things, then so be it.

Organizing my money turned out to be a pain. I had been told it was best to take American dollars as that was the easiest to exchange into the local currency. I wanted to take a fair bit, as I didn't figure I'd be spending much time near cash points once I was there. But I couldn't tell the bank why I wanted so much money all of a sudden, and they refused to give it to me in lump sums without proof of what it was for. Kind of makes you wonder whose money it actually is! So every day for a good bit I had to take the maximum out of each of my accounts from the card machine.

Meantime my spare bedroom became my kit room and I filled it with tactical gear Josh had told me would be useful, or items I had researched myself and decided could be good to have with me. I had already decided too much was better than too little, as I would rather dump stuff out there than find out I was short of something crucial. It was kind of like Christmas, with almost daily arrivals of new items I had ordered. So much so that the postman kept asking me what I was up to! I liked the challenge of finding places to get my hands on what I needed, but I have to say, it is incredible the things that can be found on eBay. Who knew I would be able to buy helmets and body armour so easily! As the pile grew, I'd stand in the room looking at my buys and feel a real sense that my future was about to change. So many of these pieces of equipment could help protect me and also hopefully allow me to help others. I was counting the days until I could get out there and make use of them.

On a Sunday evening I had to hide it all in cupboards – my cleaning lady also worked for my family, and I couldn't risk her mentioning to them what she had seen, as I still wasn't sure how I was going to tell them my plans ... I felt guilty about it though, as I have known my cleaner since I was a boy and we are good friends, so it felt like I was deceiving her.

I told my closest friends about my intentions, and reactions tended to go one way or the other, from 'Are you fucking crazy, mate? They'll stick you in an orange boiler suit, behead you for the world to see, and you've only yourself to blame then', to 'If anyone was going to do this, I should have guessed it would be you! Good on you, I wish I had the balls.'

I didn't take either reaction too seriously as half the time I felt it said more about them than me. Interestingly not one person actually offered to come with me.

I pulled together a medical kit – luckily my first-aid knowledge was pretty up to speed thanks to previous jobs – and went through all the necessary health checks. Something as simple as making sure your teeth are in good shape can prevent months of toothache on the front line. And of course I had to find out my blood type, in case I needed a transfusion. Not as easy a task as you might think, as it's not something your doctor will test for, so I had to do it privately.

I began researching courses that could train me in firearms under the guise that I was off to work in security in the Middle East. I booked on one based abroad in a forest in the middle of nowhere. I had used guns occasionally before to shoot rabbits, but I'd never used a handgun, and was keen to take a course that would teach me both pistols and rifles.

Day after day of solid shooting practice was really useful, and the trainers were great. The only time I felt bad was when we were all relaxing one afternoon, while the boss was reading his emails. He said: 'Some chap has just emailed to ask if he can come out and train with us as he wants to join the fight against ISIS. Can you imagine? Absolutely no way are we getting caught up in all that. We'd have no end of trouble on our hands.'

I squirmed in my seat and tried to busy myself, catching up with messages on my iPhone, but then realized everyone was discussing it and made a few mumbles of agreement so as not to draw attention to myself. But I felt guilty about my deception as they had been so good to me.

By the time I left the course I felt much happier about my impending trip. I may not have had anything like the expertise ex-military were going out there with, but it felt like I had a solid grounding.

I had been chatting to a guy called Rob online. He was a software engineer from North Carolina who was following similar Facebook groups to me and was also keen to go out and join the fight. He sounded like he had similar reasons to me in wanting to get involved, describing his horror at the daily images that were springing up on his computer. Rob, who was forty-four, told me he had been in the US Army in the 1990s, so I figured he would know what he was doing better than I did. His one problem was he was short of funds. I took a punt that he was serious and sent him $6,000 from my house sale money to buy equipment and a plane ticket. We agreed to meet in Dubai on 8 February 2015, and do the final leg of the flight together to Sulaymaniyah International Airport in Iraq. It is not that close to the Syrian border, but it is what YPG recommend, and we were planning to join up with

Jordan and Josh, and join a YPG unit. They tell you to go to that airport because of the safe houses en route and ally-ruled territory that needs to be crossed along the way.

One of the most important things left to do now was tell my family . . . I was dreading this as I knew there was no way in hell they were going to be OK with it. Initially I sat my mum down and told her alone. She burst into tears straightaway, then left the room for a bit, and came back and started discussing other things! That threw me, but I figured she needed to process the news in her own time. She told my dad while they were on holiday, and he texted me to say we should catch up on their return. I went over for dinner and my family tried in vain to talk me out of it, using arguments that ranged from the fact I was sure to be prosecuted when I wanted to get back into the UK to the fact that my size made me a big target. I listened to what they had to say and did my best to re-assure them, but my mind was totally made up, so that ultimately everything they said was falling on deaf ears.

Then just four days before we were due to depart, plans changed. Josh had introduced me online to Gill Rosenburg, a Canadian Israeli who was with the YPJ – the female equivalent of YPG. She had been their first Western female volunteer, and wanted me to bring out some parcels for her. She was getting some stuff sent over from Israel by people supporting her, but her country would not allow post to go directly to what they considered an enemy state, so it needed to come via Britain.

We got on well, and she was very helpful. It seemed

that she had the right mentality to be in a war zone. But four days before my flight, she told me that she had just left YPJ, and along with an American called Brett was joining a different group in Iraq, instead of Syria. She explained: 'YPJ and YPG are great on loads of levels, but sometimes their views are a bit too extreme for me. Not only that, but they have quite a lot of ties to PKK, and that isn't the best idea. We will have a lot more freedom in Iraq as we will be the first Westerners joining the group, and we can set it up the way we see fit. Would you like to join us?'

It did instantly appeal. I had wondered about the PKK association before now as well. The PKK are a Kurdish left-wing militant group who mainly fight against the repression of Kurds in Turkey and are considered a terrorist organization by Europe and America. While I think that description is not totally fair, this connection to the YPG made the lines a lot more blurred in terms of how the British government might view what I was doing. The government had made it clear that anyone going out to fight alongside Daesh would be arrested on their arrival back in the UK. How I would be treated fighting on the other side was less set in stone, but at least this new option with a group that did not have terrorist associations might make it easier for me to return to Britain.

Besides, I liked the idea of helping to form a new group, and while I realized that would involve a whole new set of problems, the idea of uncharted territory won me over.

The one thing I had known from the outset was that I

wanted to be alongside Kurdish fighters, but I hadn't been too concerned with exactly where. Having so many Kurdish friends from my time in Turkey, I knew what a great bunch of people the majority of them were, and that they wanted nothing more than to live in peace, allowed to get on with their way of life. Historically they have had a hard time, constantly having to justify their right to be anywhere, whether in Iraq, Turkey or Syria. And I think they had hoped the end of Saddam Hussein's reign would mean the end of their troubles in Kurdistan, and they could finally live in relative peace.

Kurdistan is not officially acknowledged as a country, but is a name used to describe an area across Turkey, Syria, Iraq and Iran where thirty million Kurds live, and their way of life and culture dominate. Within this, the area that has been most successful in achieving recognition is Iraqi Kurdistan, which is an autonomous region within Iraq, ultimately hoping for complete independence. Erbil is the city at the centre of this, and is the base for many of their political parties.

The Kurds' steady and peaceful move towards their own state was thrown with the emergence of Daesh, who tried to move into Kurdish territory with as much ferocity as across the rest of Iraq, getting within forty kilometres of Erbil at one point. The Kurds are a hardy bunch, though, and the Peshmerga – the Kurdish army – were effectively the last line of defence between Daesh and Europe. After the Iraqi army had fled, they had held back these tyrants on their own, and to me that proved just the kind of people they are.

This change of plan from Syria to Iraq was a nuisance on a couple of levels. The airport we were flying into wasn't brilliantly placed geographically in terms of getting to Duhok, the town where this group, Dwekh Nawsha, were based. Then there were issues such as the slightly different camouflage pattern that was worn. But none of these were major, and when I told Rob that I planned to join the fight in Iraq instead, and gave him the reasons, he agreed that it sounded like the best plan for him too.

On my last night I went for dinner in the local Nandos, and told friends I would be there from seven if anyone wanted to come and join me. Lots turned up, which was lovely. Everyone kept saying, 'Be safe, be sensible, and remember you can come home any time and we won't think any less of you!' It felt like a positive send-off. I knew I would miss them but at the same time, my mind was already withdrawing from Western life. A few friends repeatedly pointed out that I could still change my plans, but that was the last thing I wanted to do.

In fact the only time I had felt anything but total determination to go through with this was the week before. I was in the gym, on the machines, one eye on the TV, when the news came on that a captured Jordanian pilot had been put in a cage and burnt alive, with a video of the barbaric act released on the internet for all to see. It sent a shiver down my spine to think of the poor guy and his family, and I did pause to think if I really was prepared to risk putting myself and my family through that. Burnt alive in a cage – what was wrong with these people! Then anger and disgust overtook any fear, and my resolve hardened. It was deeds like this that only served to prove why Daesh needed wiping out.

After Nandos, a friend and I drove through the night to Scotland, where I left more stuff with friends, including my car, and we had a last night out drinking. I had decided that even if it was an option, I wasn't going to drink alcohol in Iraq, as I wanted to always be one hundred per cent aware of everything going on around me, and ready to act if need be.

Then finally, on 8 February, I was off. I caught the train to King's Cross, where I was picked up by a driver who took me to Heathrow, where I was flying Emirates on a business-class ticket. This was for a couple of reasons. On a nice level, I had decided if I was going to do this, I should do it in style, as it might be the last bit of luxury I would see for quite some time. But on a more practical level you had a higher luggage limit, and also booking a return business-class ticket (as I had) I figured would be more inconspicuous and raise less suspicion. Who was to know if I would use that return or not, but it at least implied I was heading out on business.

I was getting concerned about Rob, who had nearly bailed on me a few weeks before. It turned out that he hadn't told his wife about his plans to head out to the fight, and when she discovered his stash of gear in the garage, well, understandably all hell broke loose. Waiting at Heathrow, I got a call from him to say he had landed in Dubai but had taken his luggage to the wrong section, had ripped the seat of his jeans, and had run out of money. I sent him some through a money transfer shop, and hoped he would still be alive by the time I reached Dubai. I had thought it would feel better to land in Iraq with someone else, but I was beginning to wonder if that would be the case with Rob.

As I got to the gate at Heathrow the hostess held out her hand. 'Boarding card, sir?'

I paused. This was the point of no return. Once I was on the aircraft, life would never be the same again. For all I knew I would never set foot in the UK again, and I could be sending myself off to my own death in the next few months. I stood for what felt like an eternity, asking myself if I was really going to do this.

'Sir?' she gently nudged, people moving around impatiently in the queue behind me.

I looked down at the pass in my hand, and gave it to her. I was on board. Bring on the next period of my life.

Settling back in my seat I thought about fear. It is a reaction to the unknown, and there was no doubt that is what I was heading out to. But I had also thoroughly researched and prepared as best as I could, and fear was not an emotion I was prepared to allow myself to feel over the next few months. It would only be detrimental to my ability to survive, and besides, that was the emotion that Daesh thrived on in their enemy. Apprehension was the most I would permit myself, I decided. And with that settled, I tilted my chair back, and went to sleep.

2

KURDISTAN

Arriving in Dubai I found Rob standing in the middle of the departure gate looking totally lost. He was a big guy with a thick bushy beard. I'd said to him before we left that he would be better shaving it off or trimming it to fit in, but he clearly wasn't having any of that. He was friendly enough, but I didn't instantly warm to him. He seemed confused and lost in the airport, and was jumpy and all over the place. He didn't especially strike me as someone I would want next to me in a war zone. But we were on our way, and so it was time to just get on with it.

I thought we'd have a chance to get our story straight for passport control while on the connecting plane, but Rob – in new jeans bought for him by me – decided sleep was a better option. Landing in Sulaymaniyah International Airport, Rob and I were first in the queue at arrivals. I thought I was doing a good job of hiding my apprehension, but looking over to Rob I could see he was visibly shaking. Luckily the process went smoothly, our passports were stamped and we were given fifteen-day visas. This is a requirement for Kurdistan, although they would not have been considered valid elsewhere in Iraq.

We loaded our luggage onto trolleys – the combined weight of our bags was an incredible 130 kilograms – and then had to go through a final X-ray machine. All six bags were pulled to one side. Staff started going through our cases and pulling out all sorts. I had swotted up on the regulations on what could be brought into the country before I packed for the trip, so felt reasonably confident with what was in there. Items such as body armour, a helmet and Kevlar (the woven material that is used to make body armour) were all goers, but I had left out things such as the metal plates, and well, any weapons, obviously! I felt reasonably relaxed as the staff seemed mostly intent on amusing themselves with our stuff. While one guy started hitting his colleague with my extendable baton, another was trying on the night-vision goggles and a third was brandishing a machete while flinging round grappling hooks that Rob had decided it would be sensible to bring! I don't know if he thought he was off to fight in a medieval battle and we would be scrambling up castle walls, or if he was a secret ninja, but I couldn't resist taking the piss out of his choice of equipment. I wasn't laughing for long, though.

'Why are you here?' demanded a man, clearly the boss, who had been called over by one of his workers.

'We are here to fight with the Kurds against Daesh,' I explained.

'Phone someone, your Kurdish contact,' he instructed.

I tried Gill, who had been due to sort out our transport from the airport, but she and Brett were in a meeting. Speaking hurriedly, she said for me to give her a moment and she would sort something. I tried to pass on that message, but the sergeant was having none of it.

'You go home,' he dictated to us. 'Leave your stuff here, and follow me.'

Rob began to lose the tiny shred of cool that he had been holding on to, and the expletives started coming out thick and fast. 'I am here to help your fucking country, and this is how you treat us?' he raged.

The sergeant ignored him and, waving at us to follow, marched off. I couldn't believe it. We had got this far, surely it wasn't all going to be ruined now? I wracked my brains desperately for anything I could say to convince this man that we really were who we said we were. What could I do to make things all right and show we were on his side? He was behaving like we were the enemy.

Then my phone rang. 'Pass the phone to the most senior person you are with,' instructed Gill. I did, and within moments the sergeant's cocky manner changed. While I couldn't understand Kurdish, everything about his body language and manner became submissive and courteous.

He smiled at us, waved us back to the X-ray machine, and before we knew it, seats had been brought over to the security area for us, and we were presented with cups of tea. He handed my phone back and Gill explained: 'Me and Brett are with a Peshmerga captain sorting out some bits, so I asked him to have a word. He has asked your man to organize your transport. It will be a hundred per cent legit so you can relax and we'll be seeing you soon!'

The security workers cleaned and repacked our cases, and were given a cuff round the head for their troubles from their boss when he decided they were not being thorough enough. His attitude to us couldn't have changed more, and I sighed with relief.

Then, bags on a trolley, we were led through the terminal, with everyone from children to old ladies being literally shoved out of our way. It had gone to the opposite extreme, and it began to feel as though we were celebrities.

Stepping outside, the air was pretty cool – around 6 degrees Celsius. The sergeant waved a red Volvo over, and the little Kurdish driver struggled to get our bags in the car and tied on to the roof. There was nothing I could do to help as I suddenly found myself surrounded by locals, keen for a photo. It seemed word had got out around the airport about why we were there, and everyone wanted to thank us.

I was feeling great – even getting into the country was stage one completed – but having these approaches was the real living proof that the locals really did want us to be here. One of the arguments levelled at me back home had been that Westerners too often have a habit of sticking their noses in where they aren't wanted, and how was I to know that wasn't the case yet again in Kurdistan? So even this initial first impression was reassuring.

Rob meanwhile was freaking out, thinking we were going to be taken hostage by the cab driver and threatening to get back on a plane. I was struggling to make him see reason, and starting to wonder if letting him head back to the States would actually be such a bad idea . . .

We set off around 17:00, and after a quick stop for fuel and food – the sergeant had kindly paid our driver not only for the entire journey, but to feed us en route too – we were on our way.

The journey was due to be a long one, partly as we had booked the arrival airport with Syria in mind rather than Duhok, but mainly because we weren't travelling during peaceful times. The direct route was through territory currently occupied by Daesh, which understandably both we and the driver were keen to avoid. So instead we took a long and windy route through the mountainside in the safer area outside their perimeter. I looked out of the window at the wild and arid scenery. There were patches of greenery, but a lot of it was dry and dusty, and unlike any country I had visited before.

Our route took us at one point on a tiny, tight road with a steep drop to the side and no railings. While I was keeping a close eye on the cliff edge, it didn't seem to bother the driver, who repeatedly turned around to wave his phone at me, showing off videos of his son's musical talents, with barely an occasional glance ahead to keep us on the road. How ironic, I thought, if we ended up dead at the bottom of a cliff before we had even picked up a weapon against Daesh. Not the news anyone back home would be expecting to hear, and hugely disappointing to me, not that I would be around to know it!

From time to time we got stopped at checkpoints – small temporary huts at the side of the road, manned by a few soldiers with various means of preventing you from passing, from sandbags to stop signs. The guards would look in the car and demand: 'Give me your identification papers.' They would shake their heads in disgust at Rob's beard, which was really long and straggly, and as far as they were concerned was something that only the likes of a member of Daesh would grow. Amusingly, though, they would then come round to my side of the vehicle and break out in smiles. I lost count of the number of times I was pulled out of the car for photos, and the local who spoke the best English in the vicinity of the checkpoint was found and pushed forward to thank me for joining the Kurds in their fight. I think half the reason they wanted a photo was my size. At six foot two and nearly seventeen stone, I towered above the typically slighter, shorter Kurds, and they kept gesturing at my height in comparison with their own. My first experiences of the people in northern Iraq were turning out to all be positive and exactly as I had hoped.

It was getting dark by the time we pulled into Duhok five hours later, but from what I could make out it was a large town with low-rise buildings, and the shadow of mountains as a backdrop. Everything was quiet and peaceful, until Rob, who had been sleeping off and on throughout the journey, woke up. The driver was struggling to find the address, and Rob started to panic again, convinced that this was part of the endless kidnap plot. I, on the other hand, found it reassuring, as it was supposed to be a safe house after all, so if it wasn't easily found, all the better. We finally pulled up and looked out for three guys who Gill had described, saying they would be down to meet us as she and Brett were still off sorting business elsewhere.

As we waited by the car, a motley trio appeared who matched the description. There was one chap bizarrely wearing sunglasses despite the time of day, who grabbed some bags and ran back to the house. I soon learnt he was an American called Tex and was a ball of energy. Then there was a grizzly, unwashed-looking guy in a leather jacket and jeans, who I was told was a visiting reporter looking at writing a possible piece on the group. The trio was completed by the most ordinary of them, a middle-aged Canadian guy called Andrew.

Once inside we had a look around our new home. It was a gated house, with a small front garden, and the front door leading into what was called the meeting room. There was a desk and chair at one end, a sofa, and three sofas down each side. This is where we would spend a lot of our downtime, and where we all slept. There was hardly any ventilation and the smell was pretty bad. Everyone smoked in there too. After a few days I was referring to it as the room of death! We dumped our stuff there and continued the tour.

First there was the TV room where I was told the local members of Dwekh Nawsha hung out. It had a bathroom next to it, and my heart sank when I looked in and saw it was a hole-in-the-floor type of toilet. Not my thing . . .

There was a kitchen behind with a shower room attached, and it was pointed out to me that there were no real rules on electrics out there, so the washing-machine socket was almost in the shower and you had to be careful! It was a disgusting, dirty tiled room, like something out of the movie *Saw*, and every bit of my cleanliness-obsessed self was shuddering, and already planning any changes I could make to improve it. Not that we would be here for long, I hoped – the sooner we could get to the front line and get involved, the better.

Downstairs was 'the dungeon', where all the spare equipment was kept (we always kept our weapons with us), and on the first floor were a couple of offices. There was a second toilet, and I grimaced, seeing it was also a hole in the floor.

On the landing there was a table-tennis table, and then there were several offices used by the top bosses, with maps of the areas, and information sheets.

Toilets aside it seemed a decent enough place, and I figured staying here short term would be fine. We went out for food. Brett and Gill were meant to meet us, but Gill wanted to avoid the reporter. After a while we came home. Told the reporter she didn't want to do a story. He got annoyed. If it hadn't been my first day I'd have thrown them into the street, but I bit my tongue. So, exhausted from our epic journey, I crawled into bed on a sofa, no sheets. That first night I slept in the middle of the room, but the next say I set up in the corner, making my own little area.

The name Dwekh Nawsha means self-sacrifice in Aramaic, the language spoken by the Assyrian Christians. It's the language that was around two thousand years ago, so is what Jesus would have spoken too, if you believe in him.

The group was set up to help protect the Christian villages in the area in 2014, when the Daesh atrocities escalated. It was created by the APP (the Assyrian Patriotic Party), one of the leading political parties for Assyrian Christians in Iraq, and aims to fight for their rights, as well as preserving their culture, ethnicity and language. By the time I arrived there were around seventy volunteer soldiers from the local area, and then us Westerners beginning to help bulk up their numbers. The Peshmerga – the Kurdish army – were in charge of the security in the region, but Dwekh's aim was to back them up, get involved and help in any way they could. The Peshmerga, whose name translates as 'those that confront death', were not taking Western volunteers directly at that time, but were happy for them to join groups that were supporting their work.

Over the next few days I got to know Brett, Gill, Andrew and Tex better. Brett was the first there and appointed himself as leader of the group, given he had started the pull to get Westerners over to Dwekh. He was twenty-eight, ex-military, and had been based in Iraq nine years before, in the post-war time when the US Army was trying to help establish peace in the region. It was depressing for him that they had so clearly failed and we were back there now facing arguably an even bigger problem. Brett had piercings and unkempt hair and looked like he would be more at home in a festival than a war zone. A general mess seemed to follow him around. With my OCD need for order and tidiness, it quickly began to grate on me.

Brett had a tattoo on his back of the archangel Michael – the patron saint of soldiers – and was constantly reading his old battered Bible, which was full of notes and highlights. He would stay up, playing religious speeches on his laptop into the night, then not get up in the morning (ignoring his alarm).

I was also concerned about why he had decided to get involved in the fight. Each volunteer has their own deeply personal reasons for being there of course, and it is such a huge life upheaval to do so that they need to be very strongly held feelings or convictions. Brett informed me he was there as 'A soldier of Christ. This is the latest Crusade, Tim, don't forget that.'

'No it's not!' I stuttered, amazed. 'We are here to help

protect innocent people from the evils of Daesh, it is not about religion.'

I am fine with anyone's religious choice, but it should be personal to them, not something to push on to everyone else.

Besides, he seemed to see himself as being in a different camp to the Muslims, and no matter how much I tried to point out that we were in a majority Muslim country, fighting alongside Muslims, he was having none of it. Dwekh was a specifically Christian group, but the Peshmerga on the whole were Muslim. For me the Peshmerga were the bravest of the lot in the region, having battled as hard as they could against Daesh. Not to respect this, and not to see that we were all in this together, was absolute madness.

I realize that from Daesh's viewpoint religion is the motivation to fight, but in my mind – and every moderate Muslim's mind – their behaviour is not that of Islam, it is pure fanaticism. Therefore that is what we are fighting against in reality.

So I couldn't believe what I was hearing from Brett, but sadly this attitude was something that reared its head a few more times, generally with deeply Christian American volunteers. I understand that Christians are one group that have been targeted in this war, but so have many others. To turn it into a Christian versus Muslim war to me seemed very ignorant.

When I said this at any point to volunteers like Brett, I was told it was me who was being naive. Their attitude

was that Americans had suffered more large-scale atrocities than the UK at the hand of Muslim extremists, with
9/11 and then the Boston Marathon bombing, so were
better placed to judge. It really drove home that while I
often think people in the UK live in a bit of a bubble, it is
ten times worse in America, and their fear of the outside
world seems to be a strong driving force in their behaviour.

Having said that, Tex did not fall into that camp . . . in
fact I loved this guy! I quickly learned he knew all about
the politics of the region, which I had to admire him for,
as there were so many different parties and factions, but
he made a point of being very up to date on them all. He
was much more educated than Brett in that respect, and
although he too was religious, I think he was out there
mainly through a love of the military life. He was twenty-
five now, and had previously been in the US Marines for
four years, including a tour of Afghanistan, which he told
me: 'taught me a lot about life. I came back a stronger
person.' It was clear he missed that life, and being out in
Kurdistan was a way back into it for him.

Tex, who came from Texas, hence the unoriginal nickname, was a quirky comical genius who had me in stitches
from day one. I was also relieved to find out he hadn't just
been posing in sunglasses when we arrived, but had
broken his normal glasses the week he got to the country,
so was forced to wear his prescription sunglasses all the
time.

Maybe it was because Tex was such a character and I
was instantly hanging out with him, that I hardly noticed

Andrew. He was a quiet guy who at fifty-five was the oldest in the group. He seemed nice enough, although he would disappear for hours at a time, and didn't really add much to the group. He was ex-military turned painter and decorator back in Canada, and I never really got to know or understand his motives for being there.

As for Gill, I could quickly see she was a great girl with a heart of gold, who was out there for the simple reason that she was horrified by what was happening to people at the hands of Daesh, and wanted to do what she could to defend them. She was ex-Israeli Defence Forces, so had experience, and was fearless with it. She had been sentenced to four years in jail in the US after getting caught up in a telemarketing lottery fraud, but it was clear this was a period of her life she regretted, and perhaps was motivating her even further to do the right thing now. I decided that I was happy to fight alongside at least two of the five people I was joining.

It was rarely just the Westerners in the house, though. The local Dwekh boys would spend a lot of time there. As inevitably happens in these situations, the ones who spoke the best English were the ones we got on best with, and I soon became close to a couple of them in particular, Marcus and Ramen. There was also a local guy who would come and sit out the front in the daytime to guard the house. He rarely spoke, but would be there in his anorak with his AK across his lap, keeping an eye on the passers-by. I was told he had been a member of the Iraqi Republican Guard, which had been part of the military during

Saddam Hussein's reign. I was sure he had seen plenty and was full of stories, but it was clear I was never going to get any of them out of him.

There was a refugee who had recently escaped from a village under attack, who slept in the living room, and in exchange for his board would keep the place tidy, or make cups of chai whenever there were any important visitors.

I rapidly discovered that chai is like lifeblood for the Kurds. No matter how hot it is, how busy they are, how many enemies might be coming over the horizon, there is always time for a glass of chai. It is a social expectation to have one everywhere you go, so on a busy day when there were a lot of visitors, that was a lot of chai I had to drink. It is served in a glass that holds about 50ml, and at a scalding temperature, so hot it is almost evaporating. The theory is it helps regulate your temperature, so if it's hot outside, hot chai is good. But quite frankly I was always wishing for an ice-cold glass of water. We referred to ourselves sometimes as 'chaimerga' – those that face chai!

Duhok itself is a small city, with a population of majority Kurds, and quite a few Assyrian Christians, many of whom I was told had arrived there when fleeing Daesh. The people seemed relatively forward-thinking on the whole, and while they tended to stare a fair bit – it wasn't exactly like the tourism industry was thriving, so foreigners were rare – they were also reasonably friendly. Much of the time life seemed to be just ticking over, with the population going about its daily business. There was a bar, a zoo, a mall, shops serving their regular customers, even a theme park to keep kids amused. Yet it was strange to think that just thirty kilometres away people were leading a very different life, where much of the fun the Duhok residents were still able to enjoy was a distant memory. Daesh had put a stop to any of that, along with killing, destroying houses and making people virtual prisoners in their own homes.

3

GETTING TO THE FRONT LINE

The first real job I needed to tackle was my paperwork. When I landed I got a fifteen-day visa, and everything had to be put in order within that time frame. First up was getting a blood test to prove I didn't have HIV or hepatitis, as you are not allowed to remain in the country if you have either of these.

Once I had the all-clear from that, it was a case of getting sponsored by someone in a position of responsibility so I could go to the Directorate of Residency to get my residency card. Dwekh members fit into that category, so it was relatively straightforward.

I also swapped some money at this time. Many of the money shops in Duhok were more like stalls, or desks in the street with three glass windows. There were bundles of notes lying everywhere inside them, but I quickly learnt the Iraqi dinar (IQD) didn't amount to much. The exchange rate at the time was 1750 IQD to £1, so you could be walking around with a wad of notes feeling rich, when really you could probably only afford a dozen bottles of water! I was glad I had brought the dollars as it was the one currency they were keen to exchange, and there was just the one MasterCard machine in town, normally 'out of order'.

Then there was the issue of weapons. One thing I have found interesting is the number of people going out to join the fight who have assumed that they would be supplied with equipment and weapons. And paid! When you fly out, it is not like you are signing up to an army with a set structure and financing, so whether anything is supplied can be pretty hit or miss. Even with bigger organizations like YPG and YPJ, they may be able to arm you, but it will just be dependent on what weapons are available at the time. Anyone who wishes to join has to be prepared to pay their way. It means you do have to be totally serious about joining, as you are making a financial commitment, but at the same time I suppose it cuts out any capable volunteers who are not as well off. But the reality is, the Kurdish people do not have the money to fund any Western volunteer who wishes to join them, no matter how grateful they may be for the help.

Although I had been able to buy my basic equipment in the UK, I had always known I would have to purchase my weapon once I was in Iraq – it was hardly likely I would have been allowed on the plane with an arsenal of weapons. But I was shocked at the lack of weapons in my new group – one AK47, to be precise. This was owned by

Brett, and was a present from Ahmed, who was a member of Dwekh and was acting as the liaison with the Westerners. The majority of weapons were down at the front line, but I wasn't comfortable being without one here, and I wanted to have one that was specifically mine, even once we got to the front.

At the first opportunity I began asking around amongst the locals, to find out the best way to get hold of a gun. Legally you are not actually allowed to buy or sell firearms unless you have permission to do so. But it happens just under the radar, the authorities turning a blind eye as long as you don't draw too much attention to yourself.

A couple of days later some guys turned up at the house lugging a couple of bags. They told us, 'We hear you want guns?' and pulled out a couple of AKs and an RPK, a slightly longer version of the AK. Tex and I looked at them, and they were pretty shit really. They had basic pieces missing, and were the basic model, so had a wooden stock and wooden butt. It was hard to study them, though, as the locals kept taking them out of our hands, nodding, shaking and pointing at the bits they liked, and encouraging us to buy. They thought they knew better, and possibly they did, but I needed to know for myself that the key elements I had been taught on my course were all correct, i.e., the sights were in working order, the working parts moved freely, the magazine release was in working order so a magazine could be held in place, and when I stripped it down that there was no rust, the firing pin was present and the barrel was clear and intact. In the end I decided the state of the main body and the working parts of one of the AKs were in good shape, so I could fix up the rest of it. Then it was a matter of bargaining.

I had been warned that weapons would not be cheap, as with the area having been at war for so long they are in short supply. The Arms Trade Treaty introduced by the UN in 2014 also had an impact in reducing the number available. Eventually we agreed on $750 a weapon, and I got Tex his as well, after he promised to pay me back later, which he did.

Rob was interested in the RPK, which was slightly cheaper at $650, so I got him that. Then he spent the evening spray painting it and adding so much muslin to the front I was worried it would go up in flames the first time he fired it. It looked like he was off into the jungle to take out the Vietcong . . .

Then that rifle never left his side. Going to the shop to buy bleach? Rob would have his rifle on him. End of the road for a bottle of water? He had his rifle on him. When I questioned it, he kicked off: 'I don't feel safe, if I want to carry my weapon, I will.'

I was worried about the impression he was giving. Having studied how the locals behaved, it became clear that people went out and about with some weapons, but not rifles. Rifles gave off too aggressive a message, the fact you were carrying one was in everyone's face. Instead, those that could afford to would carry a pistol, but out of sight. So everyone noticed Rob and his big gun, and I was worried they would be unnerved, and think, 'Who are these guys running round town with weapons?' We were supposed to be there to improve the situation and make people feel relaxed and as though life was continuing as normal, not as though things were about to kick off and the big guns needed to be brought out. To me you take the tool for the specific job. Back home I wouldn't go to wire up someone's living-room light with a big concrete breaker, and in Kurdistan you don't carry a rifle when doing your shopping, at least not this far from the front line.

I had been warned that pistols were more expensive, as there were so few side arms about, and most of them were probably stolen from police – making it a bit of a risk to buy one as they all have serial numbers. But I decided I would feel happiest with one, so I headed for the black market, taking Brett with me. I'd been told I'd find what I needed in one of the town squares. I'm not sure what I was expecting, but when I got there I saw a bunch of old guys sitting around peaceably, drinking tea on the benches outside the cafes, cigarettes hanging out of their mouths. If it had been France I would have expected games of boules played on the dusty ground. But while it might look all friendly, they were ex-Peshmerga, and had as good a supply of arms as you would find in the area.

I quietly told a couple of people what I was after, and one came over: 'You want to buy pistol?'

'Yes, please, I'd like a Glock.'

It was the handgun I was most familiar with, and I knew it to be reliable. I had spent several days on the course shooting with it, and I had liked it. Weapons are like a car – everyone has a preference what they want to drive, and with guns you know what you like to shoot.

'I have Glock 19,' he said, opening his coat to pull one out. I started trying to take it apart.

'What are you doing?'

'I need to check it, be sure there is a firing pin et cetera.'

'No, you like, you take. $2,500.' For comparison, it would cost around $600 in the US.

'I am not happy, I need to take it apart and look.'

'No. Definitely no.'

So I walked off. Maybe the weapon was fine, and the guy was just jumpy about me stripping it down in public, but I wasn't prepared to take the risk.

I bumped into another guy called Omar, who spoke good English, having worked as an interpreter during the Gulf War. I was rapidly finding those who spoke the best English had generally filled that role, and their accent gave away if they had worked with British troops or Americans!

Omar was a slimy little character and I instantly disliked and distrusted him, but he said he could get what I was after, plus some magazines for the AKs. At this stage Brett was with me, and his loud manner meant people generally didn't warm to him. The volume level was an ongoing problem with the Americans. They don't seem to know the meaning of talking softly, or trying to blend in, and so often they marched through town talking and laughing at the tops of their voices, being brash with the locals. They meant no harm by it at all, but it was clear it put the locals on edge, and made them more wary. That was the case with Omar, who was getting jumpy about Brett, and initially told us to wait in a cafe around the corner. Several cups of coffee later, and with half the coffee shop aware of what we were doing thanks to Brett, Omar found us and said he would come to the house instead.

True to his word he turned up with a Glock for me, as well as a couple of other weapons for us to look at, including a Tariq pistol. A Tariq is effectively a Beretta pistol, licensed in Iraq as the Tariq (named after Tariq ibn Ziyad, a medieval Arab warrior who invaded Spain). They are used by the Iraqi and Kurdish police, and were the pistol of choice for the army under Saddam Hussein. The main physical difference is the Arabic inscription down the side, and Brett was instantly taken with it. Again I agreed to buy them both, on condition Brett pay me back, and after a bit of haggling, I handed over $3,500 – $2,500 for mine, and $1,000 for the Tariq.

I was very conscious that I was the one Westerner out there without any military background, and was determined that I wouldn't be the person to let the side down because of it. The one thing I knew I could contribute was money, so I was trying to be as generous with my cash as possible – whenever I saw an area where I thought my money could help, I would jump straight in.

We were still lacking rifles for the rest of the team, though, and I brought it up with Marcus, who was rapidly becoming my adviser on all things local. Even going to the shops was easier with him next to me, as I wasn't yet used to the bargaining. One silent stare from Marcus, and prices rapidly dropped!

To help with the arms problem, he took me to a house about five minutes away. We went into the garden where there was a family barbecue happening. A big fat guy came over and shook my hand, introducing himself as a friend of Marcus's, then he led me to a garage at the edge of the house. Inside he pulled back a load of sheets to reveal five AKs lying there. I looked through the weapons, taking them apart while discussing money. Outside the kids were running round playing and adults were chatting and laughing. A perfectly normal family scene except we were doing arms deals in the middle of it – surreal to say the least.

Some of the weapons were better than others, but I took all five for $2,500 and we headed on our way. I gave one of them to Marcus, who couldn't afford his own weapon at this point, and he had been so helpful to us it only seemed right. He was touched, and it felt like we were starting to become genuine friends.

I had now been in Duhok for a week, and since we were all kitted out, it was time for us to try to get to the actual front line. We spent the evening getting our weapons cleaned and in order, and our bags all packed up. I conferred with Tex on what to take, knowing as ex-military he would have a much better idea. In the end, we decided that until we knew what kind of front line we were facing the more kit we took with us, the better. Then I could tone it down when I had more of a clue about what was actually needed.

I was buzzing with excitement, and eager to get stuck in to what I was here for. It was all well and good getting everything sorted in town, but now I was more than ready to face Daesh. I had been feeling jealous in recent days knowing the locals were off manning the front line regularly.

Ramen and another one of the locals who was nick-named Selfie Steve – yep, you've guessed it, he loved taking pictures of himself – owned Toyota pick-ups. Dwekh later owned an old bashed-up truck that we eventually upgraded to a big black one that was nicknamed the Dwekhmobile. It wasn't much better, but looked a lot more serious and relevant to what we were aiming to do.

On this first day we took the pickups. They had flat backs, and Tex and I jumped into them with everyone's equipment, and settled ourselves for the thirty-five-kilometre journey to the front.

Sadly it turned out to be easier said than done. Approaching a checkpoint just a few kilometres out of town, we were flagged to a stop. A lengthy conversation ensued between Marcus and the Peshmerga guards, which involved a lot of waving in our direction and head-shaking. It turned out that as we were the first Western volunteers in the area, there wasn't any kind of protocol set up for how we were to be treated in terms of permission to get to the front line, and without instructions telling them otherwise, the guards were not prepared to let us past. Their policy seemed to be a blanket 'no' for Westerners, and it meant nothing to them that we were with the local Dwekh boys who were all allowed through fine. We were told we needed individual official clearance from a senior member of the Peshmerga, the Kurdish government.

I was so disappointed. It felt like we were offering our help, and it was being rejected. Part of me wanted to just drive through the checkpoint and ignore the guards, although I knew that was stupid. Besides, Marcus told me there were a total of four checkpoints on the road between Duhok and the front line; we would still have three more to get through, so there was no chance! But I was so frustrated.

Every few days for several weeks afterwards we would try again. We would build ourselves up. 'Right, tomorrow, let's definitely go for it,' and we'd pack everything up and get the kit in order. Then the next morning we would stop for food and petrol. When you belong to one of the local armed forces you don't have to queue at the pumps but can get straight to the front, which was always handy. Tex and I became expert at stacking up everything in the back, so we could be there relaxing on the journey, not just packed in like sardines. Not that we would ever totally relax. We would have positive control over our weapons at all times and be watching, as even in Peshmerga-controlled areas there was always a risk of ambush or attack.

But every time, without fail, it would be a 'No' from

the guard at the first checkpoint. Our rejections got so repetitive that Marcus even developed a theme tune for it, playing Lil Jon's song 'Turn Down for What', but changing the lyrics to 'turned back for what'.

A few attempts later, though, we were suddenly waved through the first checkpoint. I've no idea why – maybe they were too busy to deal with the guaranteed arguments we would put up, or they had seen us so many times they thought they knew us, so just nodded us on through. Of course then there was the second checkpoint, but that gave in to us after a few visits for whatever reason, and then the third followed suit. The sticking point was the fourth and final one, which rather than being run by the Peshmerga was under the watch of Asayesh, the Kurdish intelligence agency. We could never get past them at all. So near and yet so far . . .

Meanwhile, back in Duhok, I was finding plenty to do to pass the time. I had started hanging out more with Ramen, who was studying social science at college as he wanted to be a social worker. He was also a part-time policeman, and had a car with flashing lights and a Glock that had been allocated to him – even if it was missing its foresight after having been dropped. On top of doing all of that, he was also fighting with Dwekh, so would come home from college, change, then head to the front. He showed some serious dedication, I had to give him that. He had a huge belief in what we were doing, and would tell me, 'Tim, when you fight against Daesh, you are not fighting other humans, you are fighting bad things. It is like we are the farmers, and we have to rid the barn of the rats. That is all they are to me, rats. Their lives are of no value, so to kill one for me is not hard.'

Ramen's father, Emmanuel Khoshaba, was the leader of the Assyrian Patriotic Party, and at that time was fronting a lobbying campaign to get the Assyrian Christians their own piece of land. He was the main founder of Dwekh, and was a strong believer in fighting to defend the Christian villages. He was a big, tall and imposing gentleman, around fifty years old, who had been in the Peshmerga in his younger years. But he wasn't hands-on with our group in a military sense, more acting as its political face.

I knew Emmanuel – or Manny as he was called – socially, as my friendship with Ramen meant I would go round to his home, and he still lived in an apartment in Duhok with his parents. The first time I went there I was fully kitted up, and said I would wait for Ramen in the truck, but he told me his father would be angry if I didn't go up for some chai. It felt strange, us all sitting around drinking in their living room, me on the sofa next to Manny in all my gear. I can't imagine what would have happened if I had walked into my family's living room with an AK strapped to my chest . . . But obviously it was different out there, and I quickly got used to the relaxed attitude to weapons in Manny's house, and often called in. He would tell me about his time fighting in the war against Saddam Hussein, and showed me photos of him up in the mountains, kitted up and getting ready to go into battle.

We tried not to involve Emmanuel too much in the day-to-day issues with the group, as he had a lot on. Besides he had appointed Ahmed to be our liaison – not that he was getting results. Ahmed seemed happy to parade around with us Westerners, showing us off as though we were his prize pets, but tended to disappear when something such as the checkpoint issues arose. So there were times I would bypass Ahmed and go to Manny for advice, as after all he was the ultimate boss and provided the most chance of getting anything done. Attempting to get the permission from the Peshmerga to go to the front was one of the issues I went to him with, and he promised to look into it and see what he could do. He was an important man, so I had faith.

We grew quite close over the weeks, and at times he took on a father-figure role, looking out for me. We'd go over for dinner etc, and it felt as though he would treat us like his own family, and do what he could.

But I was hammering through my savings at an alarming rate and it did concern me just how fast my balance was dropping . . . At this stage I didn't have an end date in mind for my time in Kurdistan – in fact I had been very clear that I intended to be there until Daesh were stamped out – but I couldn't pay for myself and everyone else indefinitely. So I started considering fundraising. It wasn't something I had given too much thought to previously, but a few people on Facebook had asked about sending donations, and some of the other guys out there were already fundraising, with varying degrees of success. The general formula was to set up a PayPal account that people could donate to, and then promote what was happening out here and our aims. Then if anyone felt like they wanted to help out financially, the option was there for them.

It felt a bit strange to ask people for money, but I thought I would give it a try. I was already doing a fair bit to promote the issues through social media. The articles I had been posting on Facebook even while I was back in the UK now gave way to posts from more specialized information sites that people back home would be unlikely to come across. I would also write opinion posts, as while I was not at the front line yet, I was still meeting people who were living and breathing daily life with the threat of Daesh hanging over them.

Initially those reading my Facebook page were just close friends, but in mid-February 2015 the *Times* got wind of what I was doing, and contacted me to get some quotes on why I was there, whether I was afraid, what I was aiming to get from it, etc. I hadn't expected the story to get such a huge pick-up, but partly because of their online presence, it went worldwide. There was also the fact I was one of the first Brits to head out to fight against Daesh in Iraq, and as far as I have been able to ascertain, the first Brit who went who wasn't ex-military, which probably added to the appeal of the story in a news sense.

Newspapers, radio and TV all picked up on it and ran their own versions, or contacted me for interviews. It was crazy, and I felt that it was all a bit out of my control.

There was a weird focus on the door work I had done years before, and pictures were taken off my Facebook page and given completely unrelated captions. In one article I was called a UKIP supporter, and my name was often spelt incorrectly. But despite all of this, it was great coverage for what we were doing, and I really appreciated that the press were covering our actions in a supportive light.

Everyone warned me away from reading the online comments on the stories, but I couldn't resist, and actually found that 99 per cent of them were positive. It seemed as if a lot of people in the UK felt that not enough was being done by our government to help all those suffering at the hands of Daesh, and they were supportive of the fact I was at least trying to do what I could.

The articles meant a lot of old friends got in touch, some congratulating me, some worrying about me, and others more concerned about themselves by association. Even some of the door staff I used to work with, who you would imagine wouldn't bat an eyelid, started acting like drama queens, afraid they would be targeted. I found it interesting that people rarely acted as expected when they heard what I was up to.

Off the back of all this media coverage, I was suddenly getting inundated with online friend requests to the point that I went from 400 to 5,000 friends – the maximum number Facebook would allow, and to add anyone else had to delete someone! Then I would get people sending me messages that ranged from thanking me for doing what I was doing to asking how they could come and join me. Others, who wanted to help but couldn't or didn't feel able to come and join, asked if they could send money or packages.

Basically with all the extra followers who were there purely because they were interested in what I was doing, rather than because they were my actual friend, it felt like a wasted opportunity not to start fundraising. So I asked a contact back home to look into it for me, and they suggested that we set up the PayPal account under the name 'Improve the Situation' as that summed up my aim of being out there perfectly, and so that began.

Donations began to trickle in and we would use them to buy weapons, equipment, medical aid and food for all the volunteers. Much of the money came from the UK, but a fair bit of it came from America. I think a lot of those people came across me because I was out there with Tex, who had already developed a decent following. Gill too had quite the set of fans, and received marriage proposals on a weekly basis! Her fame had shot up before I knew her when she was YPG, and reports had emerged that she had been kidnapped along with other female fighters. They were based on false rumours started by militants on social media, but by then the press had picked up on the story, and her contribution to the war had become known worldwide.

Aside from my link to these two, there was also the fact that I was fighting with Dwekh Nawsha, and no matter what I kept saying about my own lack of religious affiliation, a lot of Americans clearly believed this was a religious war. Therefore because I was out fighting alongside a Christian militia, the more religious Americans were keen to give to Improve the Situation on that basis.

Apart from Americans and Brits, my other biggest followers were the French, and I had to dig out my rusty French and get practising, as not all of them were so great at English. This was a whole other language once it was online though, so for example I now know that MDR means 'mort de rire', or 'die of laughing' – basically the French equivalent of LOL. The things you learn thanks to war . . .

The odd Australian would crop up too. There were some Aussie volunteers out in Iraq, but they had to keep their nationality under the radar and there was no self-promotion for them, as in their country they would be punished for that as heavily as if they had gone to fight alongside Daesh. There were several other countries with similar laws too, and their volunteers were few and far between as a result, with any who did make it being sure to keep a low profile.

The Dwekh locals were really happy with the fund raising and awareness-raising that was going on, but it felt like I now had a responsibility to the group to reflect their thoughts and aims, as much as my personal ones, and sometimes there would be differences. At one stage when I wrote a big post I wanted to check with Brett that I hadn't written anything incorrect or operationally sensitive, so I got him to check it. After a few minutes of reading he said: 'It's really well written, a good piece, but add "God Bless" at the end as a sign off.'

'I'm not religious, I'm not going to,' I replied. While I was garnering support for the group, I was determined to keep my Facebook my own.

It was really interesting to see the online following unfold. The debates people end up having on my wall can be quite eye-opening, and show how differently every person sees this war. I have followers in Kurdistan who are living through this. Then there are people who come to my page with no knowledge at all, and are keen to learn. And sadly there are those who keep insisting it is a war against all Muslims and that there is no such thing as a good Muslim. I am keen to encourage open debate, but occasionally someone just has to be blocked.

As a result of the newspaper coverage, I knew the people running the arms course I'd attended would realize I'd deceived them. I felt awful about it because they had been so good to me, and they'd made it clear that they didn't want to get involved with anyone who was in the fight against Daesh. So at the first opportunity I emailed the course leader to apologize, knowing he would have seen the newspapers. He was very understanding about it and gave me some extra advice, now he knew the situation I was in.

'Whatever you do,' he said, 'don't let them capture you alive. I know it's a cliché, but you know that would be a fate worse than death, right? So if it comes down to it, and you have no other way out, make sure you have saved a round for yourself.'

I told him I had already decided that taking my own life was what I would do if it came down to it, but he continued, 'It is so easy to think that, but then in the flurry of firefight shoot off all your ammo and realize you have none left. So keep one round completely separate, on its own in a side pocket, so you never use it by mistake. Always have it on you, so if that awful moment ever comes, you know the option is there. That round is your safety net.'

What he was saying made total sense, so that night I took one round and moved it to a separate small pouch sewn onto my Osprey combat vest, away from my magazines. From then on I kept it safely there, and knew that no matter what, I had a way out of being captured. I spoke to the others and they all did the same. We would rather be dead than propaganda for the enemy.

One day a local journalist came to do an article on us. After the recent flurry of national articles that we had been involved in, we thought, 'Why not?' when they asked to chat to a few of us. We figured it could only help get more positive coverage for what we were doing. So we answered the questions and all seemed fine. Until the article appeared, that is! Incredibly, unknown to us, the reporter had taken a photograph of our house to go alongside the piece, despite knowing it was a safe house. I was furious. It was so stupid and irresponsible of the journalist and the publication. They had allowed their desire to write a good story to take priority over the safety of people's lives.

There was much discussion about what to do, and eventually it was decided we couldn't move, but needed to make the house safer. So we started making some changes to the house and installed CCTV. It was a genuinely scary thought that if there was anyone in the area keen to make a few quid by kidnapping us, the article had made their job a hell of a lot easier.

We also started stag – rotational guard duties – on top of the daily guard we had sitting by the door, so that someone was always keeping a watch out for anything suspicious, and keeping a close eye on the cameras. This went on through the night as well, and the person on duty would patrol and keep an eye from the roof.

One evening Rob was upstairs on stag. There was a radio in the guardroom, and another down in the room where we were relaxing, listening to music and sorting out our kit. Suddenly the radio crackled into life.

'Six heavily armed men heading towards the building,' Rob's panicked voice came screeching through. 'They will be at the gate in twenty seconds, react now!'

Fucking hell. We were all out of our seats like a shot, not really expecting this kind of action while we were still in town. I grabbed my rifle and headed for the front door, instantly thinking of the column just to the side of the entrance. It would give me protection, but also a good field of fire towards the gate. The adrenalin was pumping through us all – I couldn't believe someone would come for us in the middle of the town!

Tex ran up to the roof and I could see his rifle poking over the top, while the other boys spread around the building. Given that we hadn't ever practised this, everyone seemed to be taking to it calmly and effectively, and we were soon in position. If someone was going to attack us, we were ready for them. It was like my worst fear after the picture's publication, but also what I had hoped for – action!

Suddenly, 'Stand down, I repeat, stand down!' crackled through the radio. It was Gill's voice. Confused, I lowered my rifle, and knowing that I would trust what she was saying over Rob any day, I raced up to the guardroom. Everyone else arrived at the same time and we crowded in. Gill had gone there to see what Rob was looking at, and pointing to the screen, she said: 'Have a look. There are our heavily armed men.' Onscreen were six school kids walking along the road, one kicking a ball.

Rob shrugged, embarrassed and shaken. Refusing to meet anyone's eye, he muttered: 'They looked armed to me.'

The adrenalin that had built up ready for action now came out of me in anger.

'I had my safety off, ready to fire. Can you imagine if I had slaughtered all these kids? Sort your shit out!'

Poor Rob was always on full-on panic mode. I had slowly teased out of him that he had pretty much not left the States in thirty years and Kurdistan is not the place to start your travel adventures. I sometimes felt that he would have been out of his depth on a trip to London.

I know he was there with good intentions, and was motivated to do the correct thing by people, but he just wasn't mentally equipped to function out there, in my opinion. Nor was he particularly physically capable, as he was not in the best of health, and I wondered how much longer he would keep trying to make a go of it.

He was the first of so many people I was to come across out in Kurdistan who mean well, but whose presence is actually more of a hindrance to the cause than a help. Everyone needs to work out what they can do best in the fight, and for the majority of people, coming to the country may not be the answer.

One good thing to come out of that journalist exposing our whereabouts was getting to know Winston, the handyman who came round to make changes to our building. I had met Winston back in the market when I had been looking at guns, and instantly took to him. He was a proper Jack of all trades, and knew how to fix just about anything. He was motivated, creative and nothing was a fuss – just my kind of person. When I had bought my rifle I had decided to upgrade it by changing various parts, but I was having trouble getting off some of the old wooden furniture pieces. I ended up finding a YouTube video of how to do it! So there we all were, sat around the meeting room with our rifles, following the online tutorial through my iPad. But then when it came to putting on the new bits, some didn't fit as they were cheap fake versions, so we were at a bit of a loss on how to sort it. Eventually Winston came round with his bag of tools and helped us out. He had all sorts of tricks and techniques that made it easier, and resulted in a better rifle.

Anyhow, when we had been trying to make our own changes to the house security after the newspaper article, one of the guys had burst a water pipe and water had gone everywhere. We called Winston out as an emergency and he was there almost instantly. At the same time as he was fixing the pipe I asked if he could improve the shower, which was just a basic shower pan with a tap running into it.

While he was working on that he had a good laugh at our toilet. Soon after arriving in Duhok I asked Tex: 'How the hell do you cope with using a hole in the ground? I am not feeling that at all.'

To which he replied: 'I just sit on it and treat it like a normal toilet.'

I looked at him in disgust, and told him: 'Seriously, mate, I do not advise you do that. It is so disgusting, who knows what you are sitting in!'

So we got creative, found an old plastic chair, and cut a hole out of the middle of the seat, setting it over the hole in the floor. It was pretty basic. The locals found it funny, but it was better than no seat at all and definitely the lesser of two evils. On seeing it Winston asked if we also wanted a proper toilet installed, and without thinking twice I slapped him on the back: 'Hell yes!'

Brett was worried that the locals wouldn't be happy having their traditional toilets changed, but Tex told him: 'You think they prefer a hole in the ground? It's evolution, dude, it's got to happen.'

'Just do one of them,' I told Winston. 'Then if the other boys don't like it, they have the hole to use, and we have the toilet, and everyone is happy.'

Sure enough, though, as soon as our brilliant new toilet was installed, the locals refused to use anything else! So much for anyone preferring a hole in the ground . . .

At the same time I improved my life there by sourcing out a few bits and pieces of exercise equipment. No big machines, but just some weights that I put in one of the empty rooms to create my own mini-gym. With the time going spare, I was at least able to de-stress and keep in shape.

Despite all the building work adventures to keep me busy, our inability to get to the front was becoming ever more frustrating. And if I couldn't do that, I at least wanted to be doing something that would feel more hands-on in furthering the cause. The local Dwekh lads told me about work they were doing with refugees, who were being collected from the Syrian border and brought to our region. The Dwekh lads would provide armed guards to get them to the camps, or on to Erbil. Often refugees from the smaller villages had family they were able to stay with in another town or city, it was just a case of making sure they reached them safely, as the areas they had to travel through were often open to attack. Annoyingly though they never wanted us to join them on these trips.

So I jumped on it one day when Brett was contacted by a medic from America who was after an armed escort to take him around and inspect an area of Kurdistan nearer the Turkish border. He had come to the country on behalf of a medical charity that was considering working in the area, but needed to know a) where they would be most useful, and b) the extent of the security risks to all their staff.

Brett got in touch with a Peshmerga commander, who agreed to transport the medic, with Brett, Andrew and me coming along as guards. We were up early on the morning, and got kitted out in basic kit. The medic arrived at the house, and I warmed to him instantly. He was ex-forces and his company had sent lots of medics to war-torn areas before, so it was clear he knew what he was doing and would be an amenable client. We headed off in a taxi to the commander's offices ten minutes away and he drove us north from there for several hours.

At one point white tents started appearing on the horizon and as we approached it became obvious we were passing directly by a refugee camp. The tents just went on and on as far as I could see, and it was clear tens of thousands of people were housed here. There were makeshift markets set up with food and clothes, and Pesh soldiers were on duty in the camps, both to ensure the safety of the refugees and to make sure that no fighting or looting broke out within the camp.

One thing that struck me was that while the number of people was shocking, the set-up actually looked quite organized, and refugees were quietly getting on with chores, while the kids – albeit really dirty – ran about playing. It was awful that so many people had been pushed out of their homes due to the conflict, but I couldn't help thinking that those in the campsite were actually the luckier ones. They were at least alive and being cared for.

We drove on and incredibly passed a second camp, with just as many people in it. It had an almost permanent vibe, and I realized a lot of these people were bedding themselves in for the long haul. Depressingly it seemed they knew it would be a long time, if ever, before they could return to their real homes.

Our first stop was at some Pesh bases on the front line. Ironically, after weeks of fighting to get to our own front line, we just drove up to this one, although nothing of particular note was happening. The medic had a look around and chatted to some people, while we took the opportunity to let off some rounds on our weapons. It wasn't always easy to have a practice in town, but the expanse of an open area in front of us was the perfect place to make sure all our modifications were in working order. On top of that if any of the Daesh heard bullets whistling near their camp, it would be no bad thing to remind them of our presence.

The next stop was at a medical centre. Andrew and I were asked to wait outside and keep an eye out while the medic headed inside to talk with the doctors. We stopped vehicles and checked them as they passed within the vicinity, and patrolled the area. It was slightly daunting as it was just the two of us to deal with it if anything went wrong, but the idea was that our presence would be enough to put off any attacks. All went smoothly and we carried on.

On the drive back we went through to some of the nearby villages that had been involved in recent fighting. They were reduced to rubble. We stopped to let the medic get an idea of what was happening, and I got out of the vehicle and had a look around. Shockingly I could still see arms and legs sticking out from under the fallen houses, but when I looked closer they clearly all belonged to dead people, so there was nothing that could be done to help. It was particularly sad when the size of the body part or the clothing implied it was a woman or a child. We didn't know anything about the history of this particular village, but I assumed they could only have been ordinary people trying to get on with life, killed by Daesh fighters. They had probably been caught up in a raid or attack in their village, mortared as they sat in their own homes. To be caught up in a war that you had done nothing to be involved in was so heartbreakingly wasteful of human life. Again I thought of the refugees in the camp, and how there were so many people like those in this village who hadn't survived to enjoy even the small luxuries of the camp.

It was a sobering day all in all, but it gave me fresh motivation to keep pushing on with the fight. The images of those bodies, and the thought of those wasted lives, stayed with me. Everyone deserves to live a free and happy life in their own country, and all the sights I had seen that day emphasized how Daesh were doing everything in their power to stop people doing so, and sadly succeeding on a lot of levels. They needed to be stopped at all costs.

4

NEW RECRUITS

During my months researching in the UK while preparing to come out, I came across a Western volunteer called Alan who was Scottish, ex-military, and was based with YPG in Syria. I had dropped him a line similar to one I had sent other volunteers, saying that I was going to be heading out and if he had any advice it would be gratefully received.

His reply was the briefest I had been sent, and simply said: 'Are you ex-forces?'

'No,' I told him, 'but I have been planning my trip for months, am preparing thoroughly, and have been told that various groups are interested in help from non-military personnel as well as ex-military, if they show the right capabilities.'

'Don't bother coming then,' the curt reply popped up. 'Don't think I'm going to babysit you.'

'What a dick,' I thought, shocked at his response, then

I gave him no further thought until Gill mentioned his name in Duhok. She told me she thought he had been misunderstood and was intending to come and join our group. Having been plagued by a lot of wannabe volunteers online myself by this stage, many of whom were pretty clueless, I had a little more understanding of his abrupt reply.

A few days later Gill came into the guardroom and threw a patch at me with the Union Jack on it. Military kit is made with Velcro patches on the arms for badges to be attached that show your allegiances. They make a statement about who you are with, and allow people to know a bit more about your position in the battle. At this stage I was wearing a Peshmerga badge on one arm, and a Dwekh Nawsha badge on the other.

'Alan brought these for you,' she told me. 'He's downstairs now.'

I went down to find him standing in the meeting room, dressed head to foot in MTP – multi-terrain pattern camouflage, which is worn by the British forces. He also had on a Special Forces smock that was covered in Pesh badges. I shook his hand and vowed to myself that I would remain open-minded about him. Within minutes though he was trying to reorganize everyone and everything. While I knew things were far from perfect in the group and there was a lot that needed shaking up, his approach instantly got everyone's back up.

The first night Alan arrived he wanted us all to go down to the bar for a 'team meeting'. I figured a meeting to discuss the latest developments, combined with seeing what Alan might actually be able to bring to the group, wouldn't be the worst idea, so I agreed to go along.

There is just the one bar in Duhok, which is sparsely furnished with no real atmosphere, and feels more like a village hall. True to the promise I had made to myself before I left the UK, I hadn't drunk since I had gone out to Kurdistan. As far as I was concerned, spending evenings in the bar was not the reason I had gone out there, so I asked for a Coke. When Alan returned with the drinks he handed me a vodka and Coke. Either he misheard or he was making some kind of point. After a while, when it became clear we weren't going to have a serious meeting, I left them to it and went home.

Adding a new person to the group was bound to change the dynamics but I started to feel that Alan really wanted to be in charge. Fair enough, he had experience but he wasn't the only one with a military background.

There were already a lot of headstrong people in the group and there wasn't room for another. I felt that his presence was making things difficult and uncomfortable.

The atmosphere got worse when Brett and Gill fell out, which in itself was a shock as they had been thick as thieves from day one of me knowing them. To make matters worse, a few days later in the middle of the night I was woken by Tex shaking me.

'Dude, Gill has been told by a contact that her risk of capture has escalated so she's freaking out. I'm taking her to a new safe house while we find out if there is any truth to it. I hope not, but we can't risk it for now. Can I borrow your pistol to get her there?'

'Yep sure,' I mumbled, confused, and still half asleep, reaching round my side table and handing him what I thought was my Glock.

Whack! The slap round my face was accompanied by, 'That's your shower gel, you idiot!'

'Sorry,' I mumbled, dazed, and tried again.

'And some magazines now, dude?'

Whack! Apparently this time I had passed him the phone charger. Given that I kept the gun there in case of attack, particularly during the credible threat level of recent weeks, I'd like to think I'd have done a better job of finding it if a real emergency had occurred . . .

I woke up the next morning with a sore face to find Gill had gone to a safe house that no one knew about other than Tex. I had no idea how good Gill's source was – ever since I had arrived she would take clandestine calls and often referred to 'contacts' but never told us who they were. To this day I have no idea what was really going on. It is possible that the claustrophobia and the frustration of people raring to go but cooped up together was causing an air of paranoia. Or it really could have been a high-risk situation. I will probably never know! Eventually she returned, and she and Brett cleared the air too.

But while all the internal politics were starting to drive me up the wall, my biggest issue with the group was the fact we still were not getting down to the front. We were continuing our attempts to get there every few days, as well as pushing for the right paperwork. I was beginning to wonder if Manny didn't actually want us to get properly involved as I was sure he could have got us the necessary permissions, and I began to question his reasons. I know from a PR viewpoint Dwekh were happy to have the Westerners as it garnered publicity for what they were doing, and they were quickly realizing that we tended to come with funds, which were much needed.

But they were also exceptionally worried about anything happening to us. I guess if one of us had been kidnapped that would have been the worst kind of PR for them. They were particularly protective of Gill, who would get really frustrated at their constant fussing and containment of her. She knew full well that in a way she would be a bigger trophy than the rest of us for Daesh – not only because she was female, but also part Israeli – however, as an ex-soldier she knew what she was letting herself in for.

I was getting frustrated and angry, and while in some ways I felt I was learning new stuff every day about the culture, politics and way of life in Kurdistan, it wasn't what I had signed up for. I wanted to make a real difference, and so far I didn't feel that I had. So I decided to take a break and go through with my original plan of heading to Turkey for a while to stay with friends, in the hope that things in Kurdistan could improve and I would return.

*

I booked a flight to Bodrum and hooked up with my old friends. Around half the people working in the popular tourist destinations in Turkey that visitors are dealing with on a daily basis are Kurdish, not that most tourists will know.

My friends had a boat to take tourists out through the summer, and I helped them get ready for the season. I spent a good few weeks with them painting and working on it. It was mindless, back to nature type of work, and I was really happy and relaxed. In theory I had nothing serious to think about, but all the time my mind would drift back to Iraq and what was happening there, and I kept in close contact with Gill and Tex. They told me that Brett had left, with Alan going shortly afterwards to join a different group. Rob went with him, taking all the equipment I had bought him, not having repaid a penny to me, or leaving it for the group's use as I had asked him to do. I was seriously unimpressed by him, especially when it turned out later he sold it to pay for a flight home. Rob is certainly one of my biggest regrets from the whole experience – I should never have encouraged him to come, or funded any of it.

But events took a turn for the better when Gill messaged to say that Manny had told them that he was sorting out access for them. From what we could deduce it seemed that the departure of Western fighters was proving to be a bit of a shock for Manny and the other locals, and he realized something needed to be done to keep hold of us, and if possible to get me back. It was explained to him why I had left, and he was genuinely gutted I had gone. I think that was when he began to realize we were genuine when we asked to go to the front. It wasn't just pretence!

In my opinion he could have done a lot more a lot sooner. Speaking to Peshmerga contacts since, they would have been glad of all the help down the front they could get, so it was definitely a decision from within Dwekh Nawsha that had prevented that happening.

The mood of the texts I was getting off the guys changed from depressed chat about things not changing to sounding more upbeat as things started to move. And then one day the message I had been waiting on came through. The guys were off to the front line! Within days they were being allowed to stay at the base down there in a village called Baqofa, with passes that allowed them to bounce back and forth to Duhok as needs demanded. This was the freedom and action I had been waiting for.

I was enjoying Turkey, but Iraq was definitely where I wanted to be, so without further thought I got my bags packed and headed back out to join them. And sure enough, it seemed like things had improved. As opposed to the several days it had taken to get my residency card the first time, this time it took an hour.

The same afternoon I gathered all my stuff from storage and topped up any bits I needed from the market. It was strangely nice to be back. I'd got used to the people and the place on my previous visit, and it felt like a second home, something I had never really expected. Back in the safe house, I discovered there had been even more changes in personnel during my absence. Andrew had headed home the day that clearance for the front line was approved. I have to question why, when that is what we were all supposedly after, but everyone has their own reasons, and he had told the others he wanted to get married.

There were also some new guys. An American in his twenties who was an ex-US Army Ranger called Cory, a big burly Scot called JP, and an older chap from Newcastle called Jimbo. The first two were ex-military, but Jimbo wasn't, and was fresh out of civvy street. He had been a white-van driver, and despite being married and having kids – and grandkids too in fact – had been so moved by the events he had seen unfolding, he had flown out. I was interested to see how he would get on.

JP came with me to the market that first day back, and we got chatting on the way. He radiated military vibes in everything he did, from the words he used to the way he held himself. At five foot eleven he was shorter than me, but really thickset and he clearly did a lot of working out. He also had this big grizzly beard that he had grown for his time out here.

'You look like a big hairy northern beast!' I told him.

He told me about his experiences in Duhok so far, and was unhappy about how long everything was taking. He seemed like a level-headed guy, but not someone who would suffer fools either.

I said: 'Trust me, you have had it so much easier than I did when I got here!' and explained all about being turned back from the checkpoints, the endless frustrations over paperwork and the internal politics.

'Fair enough, mate,' he laughed. 'I think it has definitely improved since then. Well done for sticking it out, and for coming back!'

I added: 'I just keep looking at it as an experience, whatever happens. There are still less than two hundred Westerners like us volunteering here and in Syria, so we have to accept there is no perfect system, it will be slow, and remember it for what it is.'

Back in the room that night we kept chatting as we prepared our bags for the next day, with Jimbo joining in from time to time. The Americans sat on their beds in stunned silence, and finally, after Jimbo had told a long story, Cory burst out: 'I got three words from the whole of that, "black", "window" and "police". I am serious! How the hell am I gonna understand you guys?'

It got no easier for them to understand the Scottish and the Geordie accents as time went on, and I ended up taking on a secondary role as a translator. Whenever any of us were feeling down, though, all Tex had to do was begin his attempt at impersonating JP's accent, and we'd all collapse in laughter. I had an idea I was going to like this new combination of people better than the last.

5

THE FRONT LINE

Just twenty-four hours after I landed in the country we were heading to the front line, and no turning back this time, no, this time we were sailing through. It was funny to watch all the new volunteers complaining about how slow the journey was – stopping for papers to be checked, or pulling up at a garage for food – but for me this was nothing, we were on our way! It was now the first week of May, and with the start of summer temperatures would get up to 48 degrees in the daytime. But even the intense heat beating down on us as we sat completely exposed in the back of the truck did nothing to deter me.

When we passed that ever-elusive fourth checkpoint, I was over the moon. Finally, finally, finally, three months after first setting foot in Kurdistan, I had made it. Clearly pulling a hissy fit had its advantages! We pulled into Baqofa, which was the village set just behind the front line, and I inspected our surroundings. It was small by

British standards, more a hamlet really, primarily simple sandy-coloured detached houses, spread out with a fair bit of land between each. The area looked very dry and arid, and was very quiet.

Baqofa was about thirty kilometres north of Mosul. It was originally a village of five hundred residents, mainly Christian Assyrian farmers. During Daesh's particularly forceful blitz of Christian areas in the summer of 2014 – when I was watching events unfold from home in the UK – Baqofa was one of twenty-three villages in the area that were attacked and taken over. The residents fled to other towns and villages in Kurdistan and northern Iraq. In the autumn, though, the Peshmerga fought back, and retook the village in what was by all accounts pretty bloody hand-to-hand fighting. Daesh fled, leaving the Peshmerga to try and get the area back on its feet. It was at this point that Dwekh Nawsha was set up, to help with the work of the Peshmerga, with a focus on the Christian villages in this area.

Daesh fighters hadn't fled far, though – just to the next village over, Batnaya, hence the front line between the two. Since that time the line hadn't moved, with both sides focusing more on holding their positions than advancing or withdrawing.

Baqofa was in a very fragile state, having been under Daesh control the year before and still right on the front line. So far around twenty villagers had come back to try and build some semblance of life, but on the whole it was occupied by soldiers. In fact as we pulled up they were the only people in sight, and I quickly realized Gill was the only female in the village – something that meant she was forever having to bat off advances and flirtations. I don't know how she put up with it at times, but she seemed to take it in good spirits. Besides, she knows how to defend herself if necessary, and I think the men knew this, and never pushed their luck too far.

On arrival we were taken to a row of three simple detached houses, and told that they'd been abandoned by fleeing farmers and now commandeered by the fighters. We were to be based in the one to the right, along with the other Dwekh Nawsha boys.

The house next door was occupied by General Wahed Kovle, who is one of the lead guys of the Peshmerga. He lived there with his bodyguards whenever he was in the area. He was clearly a very important man, and apparently answered directly only to Masoud Barzani, the President of Kurdistan. Barzani had been in power for ten years, and along with his whole family was very powerful and influential in the area. The Barzanis had fought for the rights of Kurds long before Masoud was even born, and on the whole were well respected within the country. Whenever anyone mentioned the name General Wahed Kovle it was with a mix of fear and admiration. I got the idea that he was forward-thinking, fearless and completely dedicated to the cause. I listened closely to the details about him – he sounded like an interesting guy, someone it would be good for us to meet. It was this general who had signed the paperwork to allow us to the front, so we owed him already, and if he could open those doors so easily, who knows what else he might be able to get us involved in.

The third house contained members of the Peshmerga, in particular the Counter-Terrorist Group.

We soon settled into our base, although it was even worse equipped than the house in Duhok. All the Western-ers had to share one bedroom, which within a day or so was dirty, stinking and far too hot. The toilet, although theoretically a self-flushing one, was not working, so we had to chuck a bucket of water down it after every use.

The idea was to remain in Baqofa as much as possible, with trips to the nearby village of Al-qosh for basic sup-plies, and occasional visits back to Duhok for larger supplies, to shower, clean up and have a break.

We quickly fell into a routine. We were asked to do stag duties, mainly keeping watch from the roof of our house. Some of the others found this boring, but for me it was a total novelty. From the roof I could actually see the front line, a mere seven hundred metres away.

It helped that Marcus was in charge of putting together the rota for stag duty, and he would always make sure that either he or Ramen was on with me, as we all got on so well.

Marcus is a pretty fascinating character. Originally from Baghdad, his father had fought in the Gulf War on the side of the Iraqis. That we were able to be friends, despite the history, proved how much politics had changed in those intervening years, but also that he was open-minded and a realist. Marcus, who was twenty-five, had come to join Dwekh Nawsha out of a sense of humanitarian duty. He was also a deeply religious Christian, and had worked as a minister before we had met, but he handled his religion in a way I admired – quietly but sincerely. His life was clearly directed by his beliefs, but he was aware that I wasn't interested in it, and accepted that. He never tried to discuss religion with me, and told me he liked that I was honest, and not pretending to be something I wasn't, so he knew where he stood. He had concerns that some of the other Christians didn't follow the religious principles they claimed to live by.

As a soldier I felt Marcus was dependable, and of the local Dwekh boys he was the person I was most happy to have at my side. He had grown up around war, so had a realistic idea of what it entailed, and had still chosen to get involved.

Marcus's nickname was Zombie, as he would sleep all day, be awake all night, and perhaps as a result of that had skin so pale we joked he looked more Western than the rest of us! You could joke with him and piss about which was one of the reasons I liked doing stag with him. He also thought nothing of spending hours in companionable silence, which works for me too. Marcus would get frustrated with the Americans' constant need to fill the silence with chat, so would hunt me out to spend time with instead.

We were also asked to take on duties patrolling the village, which I really enjoyed. The idea was to reassure the few people living there, but mainly to make sure no Daesh had slipped across the front line undetected, and were hiding out, or had left landmines.

I had never been taught how to patrol, but I am not sure it is something you necessarily need training in. Not to say that there isn't a hell of a lot of military training that teaches people techniques far beyond anything I have picked up, but with something like patrolling, a lot of it is common sense.

It was one of the interesting aspects of life in this war. In some respects the ex-military guys were much better equipped than I was, but in another, they were at a disadvantage. They were so used to having a full army to back them up, and a boss to tell them where to be and what to do, that in situations where you have to think on your feet and for yourself it was perhaps easier for me as a civilian.

In the case of patrolling it is about being observant, opening your eyes and ears, not kicking big lumps of concrete in case they are IEDs . . . And being polite, especially in civilian areas. The few remaining farmers and those who had returned to their homes in Baqofa were all afraid, and didn't always trust that the guys at the front line would stand their ground. So it was part of our job to encourage them to have faith, and to feel as secure as possible in their own homes. We would also visit surrounding villages and do the same there. They were all Christian villages, so their fear of being slaughtered was particularly high, which was understandable. The track record of

Daesh was to show very little mercy to Christians, be they men, women, or even children.

Shortly after arriving in Baqofa, Tex and I tried to call in on a good friend of his from Dwekh who he knew from back in Duhok, but when we went and knocked at his house, there was no reply. It turned out he was in the hospital, having been bitten by a donkey! There was a poor mangy creature who lived on a bridge on one of the roads in the village. I imagine his owner had fled when Daesh had taken the village, and somehow he had survived ever since. When I first saw the donkey, I commented that it would have been kinder to have despatched him, and put him out of his misery. He was skin and bones, dirty and limping. Although as it turned out, clearly there was still some life left in the poor creature.

Despite the twenty-four-hour look-outs and patrols, it was theoretically possible for people to get across the front line. The shortage of night-vision goggles, combined with straight-up human error, meant that skill and luck could get an enemy behind our line.

One evening we were all relaxing in our bunk room when we got a shout from Ahmed. I had been watching *Fawlty Towers* with Gill, a habit we had got into, as she loved it, having watched it when she spent time in the UK. But we dragged ourselves up and headed downstairs where Ahmed told us that suspected Daesh had been seen in the area and everyone needed to go and investigate. Instantly geed up, we got kitted up and headed out, and saw that the Pesh were also out en masse, everyone wary and on edge, keen to be the first to spot the enemy.

We looked around nearby buildings and checked down alleyways, inspecting the ruins of houses and behind compound walls, but nothing. Then Jimbo appeared with JP's night-vision goggles. He fell into line behind me, with the guys in front and behind walking quietly, everyone focused on their job. Suddenly Jimbo stopped, and hissed: 'There are people in the field!'

Word quickly went up and down the line and we all took up defensive positions, down on one knee, weapons cocked, watching, and holding our breaths.

There was no movement. 'Jim, what exactly can you see?' I whispered.

He was still studying the area through the goggles. 'There are eight or ten guys in that field. They are crouched down and staying still, but they are definitely there.'

Marcus came up behind us quietly, and after scanning the area for a bit, announced: 'There is no one there, I am sure of it.'

He turned away and Jimbo passed me the goggles for a look. True enough I saw a movement in the field and tightened my grip on my rifle. Marcus was wrong. Or actually, was he . . .

'Jimbo, put your right arm in the air. Wave.'

He looked at me like I was crazy, trying to make him into a target. But I was adamant so he did it. There was movement out in the field. I lowered the goggles.

'You are seeing our shadows caused by the light from the buildings behind. If there are Daesh out there tonight, it is not in that field. Sorry, mate,' I said, reapplying the safety catch on my rifle. Then seeing his dejected and embarrassed face, added: 'You've not used the nods before, I'm sure I could have made the same mistake.'

'We've all been there, let's not worry about it too much,' added JP from behind Jimbo.

Ahmed was still sure the intel on the initial sightings was good though, and asked us to keep looking elsewhere in the vicinity. So this time we decided to set up on the roofs of two large villas that had clearly been at the point of nearing completion when the owners were forced to flee the village. The structures were finished, the concrete skimmed, but no furniture or decoration had been inserted. Instead they stood, a mirror reflection of each other, with just a couple of feet between and a wall around and dividing them, creating courtyards and effectively their own mini compound.

We decided to call the houses Alpha and Bravo to differentiate, with the Brits heading to Alpha roof, and the Americans to Bravo, with a couple of the local lads joining each team. JP and Cory stayed on the ground and headed for the undergrowth to cover us into the building, with the aim of joining us afterwards.

Jimbo, Marcus, another local lad and I went in to Alpha, checking the rooms one by one, covering each other and communicating by pointing rather than words.

We kept the operation quick and straightforward, so that in no time we were on the roof.

It was a distinctly different operation next door. The way they were carrying on you would think the American Embassy in Iran had been taken over again. There was a lot of effort and shouting going into clearing each floor, then there was all the high-fiving, back-slapping and 'yeah buddy!' when they reached the roof . . . Marcus and I just looked at each other and shook our heads. It was clear the Americans' attempts to demonstrate their building clearing tactics was not impressing anyone except themselves.

We explored the roof, which was flat and had a great view out over the surrounding area, particularly to the south in the direction of the enemy. There was a waist-height parapet wall running around the perimeter where it was easy to secure yourself behind. The only thing to be careful of was one gap in the wall that hadn't been secured – that and the rubbish all over the roof. Some of this was metal bars left over from the building work, I guess, but it was the plastic bottles that were the biggest problem. The country is polluted with empty plastic water bottles. People drink from these ridiculously tiny little bottles, get through them in a few mouthfuls, and because there are no bins, they just drop them. It is rare to see someone even bother to throw it to the side of the road. Just there, in front of you, minimal effort, seemed to be the way to dispose of rubbish.

Anyway, after we were sure it seemed clear, and

nothing was to be seen in the surrounding areas bar several members of the Pesh who were still patrolling below, I radioed down to JP: 'Head yourselves up.'

JP and Cory gave the thumbs up and started walking round the corner of the building. I went back to sorting my gear when there was a sudden burst of gunfire from below. Fuck! I ran over to the wall. The Daesh trespassers must be just below us!

'It's us! Stop firing!' JP yelled, from the wall he had dived behind.

The shots petered out, and it turned out some of the Pesh had seen a couple of guys, hadn't instantly recognized them and had opened fire. It just showed how jumpy everyone was that evening. It was exceptionally lucky they had bad aim and the bullets had sprayed a foot or two off target, or that would have been the end of JP and Cory. We spent the night there, worked till first light then went back to the FOB.

Just two nights after we first went up onto the roofs of Alpha and Bravo, Ahmed called round to see us, to say Peshmerga bosses were estimating the chances of attack that night as 70 per cent, and the General, who had arrived after manning the front lines elsewhere, was keen for us to get involved. Thank fuck for that!

Ahmed agreed that Alpha and Bravo roofs would be good places for us to be stationed, and we could cover the area well from there.

'Right,' I said, instantly motivated. 'Let's split into two teams, Brits and Americans like last time with a few local lads with each of us. Take everything you possibly can up there, firearms, ammunition, the lot.'

We decided we needed someone to take charge of the mission to give it some semblance of order and stop it descending into chaos, and Cory volunteered.

I had a lot of time for Cory, who had plenty of military knowledge. He had a thorough understanding of the politics of the region and was always looking ahead to when Daesh were dealt with, concerned that new fanatical groups would emerge to take their place. I was forever saying to him, 'Let's deal with this problem, and look at the next one down the line,' but it was no bad thing to be so forward-thinking really. To be honest, sadly, I am sure he is right.

Anyhow, Cory decided that we needed to walk the route from our house to the buildings in tactical formation, in this case, a staggered column. This means walking in two lines with everyone evenly spaced and staggered, so effectively forming a zigzag pattern. The theory is that it works brilliantly from a defensive point of view, as it gives everyone a clear arc of vision and field of fire.

We met at 20:00 and got into order, before setting off down the road. Although I hadn't done this kind of tactical movement previously, it made sense to me and I grasped it pretty quickly. A bit of me felt like it was over-kill for such a short distance, but at the same time I figured it did look professional, and you never know when it might become necessary.

The problem was, while the Westerners may have seen the sense in it, the locals had no interest in it at all, and thought we were mad. We tried explaining to them what we were to do, but they were all over the shop as we set off. One would be chatting on his phone wandering off the side of the road, while another was too busy eating a Slush Puppy to watch where he was going. When one ran back for his can of Red Bull, and another said, 'Fuck it,' and jumped in his truck to drive there, I nearly gave up! But we pushed on nevertheless.

Separating into our buildings, the Alpha team quickly reached the roof – just in time to hear the Americans next door call: 'Ground floor, clear!' It seemed like they were sticking to their guns on their routine then, despite the ribbing we had given them after overhearing their last house clearance . . .

On our roof was JP, me, Jimbo and Marcus, and we were joined by three of the other local lads, Big K, Sticky and Ramsay. Big K wore cammo all the time and had a massive belly, so we thought he looked like a kebab. He didn't speak too much English though, so I am not sure he even understood his nickname. Sticky gained his name due to his habit of nicking anything. He would come into your room to chat, you would think you had enjoyed a nice conversation, then five minutes later when you were looking for your ammo you would discover Sticky Fingers over there had 'borrowed' it. He could never understand what was wrong with that – his attitude was that everything belonged to everyone. At least when it suited him! Ramsay was a really little, really angry chef, who – you've guessed it – was named after Gordon Ramsay.

I set myself up in the south-east corner of the roof to get a view out in both directions, and so that I would have the protection of two angles of wall. I got all my equipment set up for easy access at a moment's notice, and made sure I always had my weapon within arm's reach. Jimbo was along from me on the southern wall, and then there was JP, who was setting up with the night-vision goggles to survey the area. The other three were spread across the back, northern end of the roof, which concerned me slightly as any firefight was more likely to be to the south, and well-meaning friendly fire could easily hit me in the back.

Then, I'll be honest, I don't know what happened. The whole evening began to turn into farce, like something out of *Dad's Army*.

It all began with Jimbo.

'Tim, mate, where's your rucksack?' he shouted over. 'Can I borrow it?'

'What for?'

'I want to put it against the wall so no one treads on my iPod speakers.'

'Sorry, mate, but what the fuck?'

Now no one can sit in total silence all the time, I realize that, but noise as far as I am concerned should only be necessary if it is connected to the mission. Just before this

I had been reminding him to speak softly and take the bass sound out of his voice, as that is the bit that will travel.

A minute later, despite my incredulous response, Elvis Presley started singing. At the same time, Jimbo got on the phone for a Skype call with his missus.

'All right, love?' he said. 'I'm on the front line waiting for an attack.'

It felt so mundane and surreal that for a split second I wondered if I really was in Kurdistan and not back on a construction site in England. I found myself glancing over at JP to check. Yes, there he was, ammo loaded, ready to go. He caught my expression and just shrugged.

'Each to their own,' he said.

I debated saying something more to Jimbo about the music but didn't feel I knew him well enough and didn't want to upset him. He just did his own thing on the whole, occasionally coming out of his shell to chat about his dogs back home or the grandkids. He had proven himself to be a nice lad, but wasn't one for lengthy debates.

Meantime Big K was sitting on his haunches, moaning and groaning, and whispering (so in that respect he was doing better than Jimbo) to Marcus, who then came over to tell us: 'Big K is ill. He has food poisoning and is going to shit himself.'

Who knows if he was, or he thought that things were really going to kick off that night and he didn't want to be involved, but either way it was clear he wanted off that roof.

'Have you used a radio before?' asked JP, raising his voice to be heard over Jimbo's music, which had now moved on to Neil Diamond's finest hits.

'Of course,' I said. Between door work and the prison service, radios had been part of my regular daily equipment.

'OK, cool, you are in charge of comms. Get on the net, speak to Cory, and tell him we need one of their people over here to relieve Big K. They have an extra man.'

Then JP asked me to come and take over with the night-vision goggles. He was given them by a member of his family and they have a lot of sentimental value for him, so he is very protective of them. JP would never just set them on the wall in case they got knocked over. I headed over in the pitch black, but suddenly tripped over an unseen obstacle, hearing something scatter over the roof. Grabbing the goggles I looked down in the blackness to find out what was at fault, and could see magazines everywhere. Jimbo had taken all his magazines out of his vest, and packed them in a neat pile.

'If you leave your magazines in your vest, your ammo will be instantly to hand, even if you have had to make a dash for it,' I said quietly to him.

As he picked the magazines up I glanced around at the others – Ramsay was playing Candy Crush on his phone, while Sticky was wandering around the roof shiftily, no doubt looking for the latest thing he could add to his collection of 'borrowed' property.

Shaking my head I turned back to scanning the area

around us with the goggles. No matter what, I at least, was going to try and do the job I was here for . . .

A bit later on, JP tried to call over to Bravo roof to check on some equipment. There was no reply, and I tried calling over to them on the radio, but with no luck. Ducking in close to the wall we could hear a selection of snores and deep breathing. Although they would deny it later, they were all fast asleep. Incredible. Turning to JP, I asked: 'Is it really so difficult? Do your job. That is all each person needs to think about, but for whatever reason tonight it seems no one is capable of that.'

At 03:45 we started getting ready for the dawn stand-to. Stand-to means being on high alert for action, and just before sunrise and just before sunset are the times of day considered the most likely for an attack to happen. We agreed between us that we would treat this as though it ran until 06:00, and suddenly everyone was serious again.

'Knock the music off, mate, this could be it,' JP said to Jimbo, who duly obliged and also brought his magazines back close to his side.

You can see the very first light of sunrise appearing on the night-vision goggles. They work by gathering all the ambient lighting and magnifying it to help build a clearer image. It is tinted green, as the human eye can study that for longer periods of time without getting tired. Something as bright as the first glimmer of light on the horizon is very clear through the glasses, but as more light appears they become useless.

I was pumped and on edge. Although I had been on stand-by all night, I had taken the odd turn at lying down to rest my legs and arms. But now I was full of adrenalin, desperate for the action to happen.

By 06:00 am though there hadn't been a single movement on the horizon, or the slightest sound. Nothing had happened, and with a heavy heart I agreed that we should call it a night. We packed up our gear and met Bravo team in the courtyard. They looked like shit with dried saliva down their faces and helmets on one side. Hardly an elite force. We walked back in a half-hearted attempt at formation, with even the locals in better order as they trailed behind en masse.

As we got near the bridge, I looked up to see the donkey in the middle of the road and nervously unclipped my rifle from its sling. I didn't want to hurt the poor thing, but if it tried to attack me I would definitely rather bash it than let myself be bitten. I had not forgotten Tex's friend's nasty gash!

JP couldn't stop laughing. 'Mate, you are a non-military person yet you were fearless on the roof, geed up, buzzing and ready for action. And now look at you, terrified of a helpless animal!'

'Too right,' I retorted. 'Although there is nothing helpless about this vicious donkey. Besides if I have to fight it off, it'll be the most action there's been all night!'

I have no idea what was in the bottles of water that night, but it had been a farcical outing. Luckily that wasn't always the case, because if the guys were like that every night ... well I'd have been long dead, and not around to write this book!

6

ACTION!

After ten days of settling into our new home and getting into the routine of stag and patrols, JP and I spoke to one of the Peshmerga commanders who worked for the General.

'Are we able to come to the front line with you one day and help out there?' we asked.

He seemed surprised, and said that Dwekh had given the impression that we had wanted to stay back from it a bit, but if that was what we wanted, we were more than welcome. This news did not surprise me. Back in Duhok I had come round to the belief that Manny wasn't keen for us to be on the front line and be too closely associated with Peshmerga, and I had repeatedly seen it in Ahmed's behaviour, in blocking our desire to be as close to the action as possible, phone calls which he refused to translate, etc.

The Peshmerga commander told us to meet him later

that day. He would take us to the front and we could spend a few hours working under an officer called Rad, who was a captain, and effectively one of the General's seconds in command. He warned us that it didn't look like anything too exciting was expected that afternoon.

'The majority of the action happens at night,' he explained, 'as it is too hot in the summer months for either side to want to be out in it, however we haven't had any intel about expected action either this afternoon or tonight. It's not a hundred per cent accurate, but you can generally go with it.'

That was fine for me, as it would give me a chance to familiarize myself with the area and how things worked up there.

We went back and told the others, and we all got our kit in order, and waited as instructed out the front of the house. We jumped into a Peshmerga vehicle with our new friend, and headed up to the front line, a mere seven hundred metres away from the houses.

This was to be the outing that I described in the prologue – the day I got to see Daesh and my first front-line action!

After everything we had been through to get to the front line, seeing Daesh just across the other side of no-man's-land sent a real thrill through me. And then for the mortar rounds to start falling, it was as though things were beginning to take place as I had imagined. But once I was lying in the dirt waiting, time dragged to the point it seemed like I was there forever. The 48-degree sun was burning down on me, and the sandflies were out in their hundreds, with what seemed to be the sole aim of biting the shit out of me. As I shook out a leg to try and get rid of the cramp, I looked over the berm, but there was no sign of movement.

My phone pinged with a WhatsApp message from Gill, who was stationed behind sandbags along to my left with Cory and Marcus, checking in that I was OK. This was one of many thousands of WhatsApp messages I exchanged with people from the front line. As a method of communication it is much more secure than text or calls, and allows for group conversations about everything from equipment requests to directing mortar fire. Although who would have thought you would get WiFi on the front line. This was modern warfare at its finest.

After a bit I glanced over to the right, where three locals were looking out from their observation post at the end of the trench, about twenty metres away. They beckoned me over to join them. It was tempting to be around other people for a bit, and besides, I was keen for a chance to stretch my legs. I looked around and seeing no movement, decided, 'Fuck it,' and jumping up I ran as fast as I could to join them, thinking, 'Please don't let me get slotted right now!' Running up the bank just in front of them, I dived straight in without looking, and sent plastic chairs flying, laughing with the sheer adrenalin of it.

They greeted me, and incredibly signalled for me to pose with them for a selfie. There we were, in the middle of a battle, and their priority was pictures. All I could do was laugh. So I stood against the back wall, but no, they pulled me to the other side – it seemed we needed the enemy behind us. It was surreal, grinning away to a camera with three men I had just met, in a dirt hole with mortars falling behind us.

JP radioed down, laughing again: 'Mate, that was some swan dive you did into the trench! Are you all right?'

He said that from what he could see the action was slowing up, but that Rad had said to give it a bit longer. So I settled into one of the plastic chairs, following the lead of my three new friends. A fourth guy appeared along the trench carrying a tray with water and chai on it, and handing it to me, headed off again. Then for half an hour we chatted away, the locals talking Kurdish, me talking English, and none of us understanding a word of what the other said. I realized I was really quite happy though, and enjoying myself. Except there were mice, rats, bugs and flies everywhere – in your kit, etc. Along with sandflies, they became as much my enemy as Daesh!

From time to time I would look over the edge of the trench and use the binoculars to scope out the area and check for movement, but the horizon was still. One more mortar fell and I ducked with the sound, but the others didn't flinch and signalled that it was nothing to worry about.

Eventually Marcus came over and said the captain wanted to call it a day. He took me to an old agricultural shed where the others were gathering to have yet more chai, and to cool off thanks to the air-con units that had been set up in there to blast out cold air.

I analysed the afternoon with JP, and discussed everything I had done to get his advice on what was a right and a wrong move, and to improve for when the next day like this happened.

The only Westerner who hadn't come down to the front line was Jimbo. When we told him about the green light we had been given to be there that day, he replied: 'I go to the front when required. I am out here as a defensive force.'

It was a fair enough position to take, and there was definitely work to be done back in Baqofa, but if I was Jimbo I'd have felt cheated. Out on the actual physical front line was exactly where I wanted to be.

I looked around at the other Peshmerga in the building. A couple were clearly new recruits of about seventeen years old, who looked terrified, and were holding on to their weapons really tightly, even now we were stood down. I realized one of them had his Peshmerga patch on upside down, so sauntering over and shaking his hand I subtly straightened it for him. I really felt for him, thrown into a war as horrific as this when he was still a kid.

It started getting dark, and the captain came over and, speaking in good English, said: 'We have done dinner for you, come upstairs.'

'No, we have to get back,' butted in Ahmed, who had appeared in the last hour.

'Everyone will be offended if you leave,' the captain

said. 'Besides, once it is dark, we can go back on the roof and use the night-vision goggles.'

No way were we leaving on our first day at the front line! We followed the captain upstairs, where we ended up sitting on the concrete floor while Gill got the most comfortable seat. I took the piss that being female had at least that one advantage down in Baqofa. Our meal was 'lamb', as it is often called out there on menus, but is actually goat. Everyone kept apologizing for the quality of the meal and saying there were no good shops nearby, but as far as I was concerned it was hot meat and rice, and a can of Coke, so I was more than happy.

'What do you think of the war?' 'Which of your countries are going to get involved?' 'What do you think Daesh are going to do?' 'Why are there people coming from your countries to fight on the side of Daesh?' The questions kept coming from the soldiers who could speak English. I avoided answering until someone asked me a direct question, and I replied: 'Honestly? I don't know and I don't care too much about the politics. I just know that Daesh are extremely bad people that shouldn't be able to do what they are doing, so I am here to kill them.'

The captain cheered and gave me a slap on the back – a move he regretted when his hand hit the tough metal of the weapons I still had tucked in there.

I wasn't saying this to impress Rad, I really did try and keep things as simple as possible. I didn't want to get bogged down in the rubbish that people would end up arguing over, but focused on what was good versus what was bad, and that was it. I used to explain it as 'No RPG', that is to say no religion, no politics, and no gobbledy-gook. What I really meant was no religion, no politics, and no bullshit, but RPB doesn't really have the same ring to it!

'We'd better get back,' Ahmed told us again, using Marcus to translate.

'Why?' I asked.

'Well, we have been up here a while.'

That wasn't a satisfactory answer for me, and turning we all blanked him and carried on our conversation. A bit later we headed onto the roof and kept watch for three hours with the night-vision goggles, but it seemed all the action for that day had been used up. Still, I went to bed that night a very satisfied man.

Trips to the front quickly became part of our routine. We would go down there overnight, sleep in the morning, and then go on patrol, prepare kit, do general chores and relax during the afternoon.

We had recently learned that Daesh had put a $150,000 bounty on the head of any Westerners in the area who were caught dead or alive. I knew an amount like that could turn people who until now I had felt were trust-worthy. A poor local guy with no strong allegiances in the war might think this could be an easy way to make a quick buck, but it was just another cowardly move by Daesh.

I realized this was just more of their propaganda, Daesh trying to flex their muscles and win through perpetuating a sense of fear, rather than winning the physical fight. Good luck to anyone who wanted to try and knock me over the head with a rock in the night. We were too well prepared for that.

After our initial concerns, we dealt with it by joking about it. 'Why is Tex valued at the same price as me?' I would demand angrily. 'There is a third more of me in body size, so I should be worth at least $200,000!'

Tex meanwhile decided to use it to taunt Daesh, and on a couple of occasions he would stand at the front line, waving his four-foot American flag, shouting at the top of his voice: 'There are four Westerners sat here right now waiting for you, so that is $600,000. What are you waiting for? Come and get us, motherfuckers!'

In military terms Tex is unflappable and fearless. He would have loved nothing more than if that had got a rise out of them and brought on a firefight. When it didn't happen, it made us see their bounty as even more ridiculous.

I was fascinated by Tex and his behaviour. He was one of the funniest guys I have met, but also deeply military. That way of life was ingrained in him as he had been in the US Marine Corps from twenty to twenty-four years old, coming to Dwekh shortly after leaving. He would be so caught up in his own world that he would think nothing of dropping to his hands and doing press-ups in the middle of an important front-line briefing.

ACTION!

He was constantly full of energy and a need to do something. He chewed dips all the time, a dry tobacco that Texans stick in their mouth between their lower front lip and gum. The grim bit of this was it made him constantly need to spit. It meant that there was a plethora of small water bottles lying around the place with spit in them, which I found totally disgusting. One day I noticed one of these small cans of dip had a green string hanging out of it.

'What's that?' I asked Tex.

'Don't touch it!' he replied quickly. 'It's a homemade explosive!'

It turned out Tex had been collecting all the propellant from damaged rounds, and storing it in a big glass jar with the idea of making fireworks. I wasn't sure it was the best idea, but when Tex got something into his head, it was best to leave him to it.

One afternoon soon after, we were sat around near the house, relaxing and cleaning weapons, while a few of the Pesh were on patrol. Suddenly there was a huge bang right by the General's house, and everyone jumped up and straight into action. Pesh appeared out of nowhere and everyone was making their weapons ready, wondering what had been fired and from where.

There was lots of shouting, but Tex's voice rose above them, laughing: 'It's all right, everyone, I was just blowing up a firework.'

For fuck's sake. We were in a war zone and he was

doing that. I had to laugh, though – he had made some of the locals move faster than I had ever seen before!

Shopping in Al-qosh was a strange experience. While it was a functioning village, it didn't have the distance from the front line that allowed Duhok to carry on with everyday life as though things were fine. So here Pesh would walk around with their weapons – there was generally a more military feel to it, along with checkpoints. I would arrive at a shop and there would be several lined up outside the door, Dwekh or Pesh had set them while they were inside shopping. I would never have left mine alone, obviously! At other times I would get a lift off a local, and had to shift several AKs off the front seat before I could even get in the car. Men carried a weapon around the village as casually as though it was their wallet.

On one occasion a local stopped me and asked if his son could hold my gun. Such a bizarre request, but I knew enough of the culture by then to know it would be an insult to say no. So instead I took the magazine off, cleared the chamber and handed it to him.

Another day I had missed my lift back to Baqofa from Duhok, and getting into a taxi with my bags of shopping, I hesitantly asked the driver to take me to the front line. He didn't bat an eyelid, and set off. War is such a way of life even for those living a bit back from the front line that for him there was nothing bizarre about my request. In fact the driver refused to take my money, as many of them did, instead thanking me for being out there and helping in their fight.

During one of the afternoon patrols we got a new addition to the team ... Marcus and I were on a routine check of the village, and headed into an abandoned courtyard. Marcus kicked open the door of the house and jumped back, as what looked like a large rat ran out. The rats out there are huge, and not something you really want to come across, but this one made a beeline straight for me.

I jumped back in horror, all ready to unload my gun at the filthy creature, but just in time realized it was actually a tiny puppy. He rolled round at my feet, a dirty, malnourished little black bundle of fur. He was so clearly desperate for attention that I scooped him up, and decided to take him with me, just for the patrol at least, as it was clear he wasn't about to go off and do his own thing anyhow.

Marcus shook his head in disbelief as I petted the poor little creature. Out there so many people are struggling just to survive that their main focus is to give the humans a decent life. Understandably they don't pay much attention to animals in general, or set much store by their lives. As such there are a lot of strays generally doing their own thing, and not too fussed by people. We already had one semi-adopted dog back at the compound, a stray called Julie who had wandered in and ended up staying. We finished our patrol and got back to the house, where I set my new friend on the grass outside, and went in, saying, 'Bye, little fella,' thinking he would be off, and that would be the end of it.

A few hours later I went back out, and there he was waiting for me. So I got him some water and food scraps, which made him more excited. He was jumping all over me, and he was so filthy I thought I had better give him a bath. I went through three big whole basins of water before I was satisfied that at least the majority of the grime and mud was off him – and then realized to my amazement that he wasn't an entirely black dog, but had white and tan bits that had been impossible to see before! I decided he was probably a sheepdog cross.

The next morning he was still there, and I decided to name him Rocky. Before I knew it my afternoons – which are the dead times – were spent in the garden with him, playing with him, feeding him, bathing him. The other boys took to him too, and were very protective of him. JP would wander upstairs to tell me: 'Your dog has been bathed, fed and watered.' Even Marcus softened towards Rocky after a while, and I would occasionally catch him giving him a bath in an effort to get the ticks off him, or find him playing with him – even if there was an element of torment to it, such as balancing an ammo pouch on his head!

Occasionally Rocky would sneak into the house when it was really hot, and hide under a bench or table to enjoy the air conditioning, or if he was really cheeky, we would find him up in the bedroom.

We kept meaning to get into town and get hold of some proper dog food, but we never got a chance so instead he lived well off our scraps of meat, chicken bones, pasta and his favourite food of all – Dairylea triangles! Funnily enough when I put his picture up on Facebook I had more offers from people wanting to send stuff out for Rocky than I ever had for the boys. People wanted to send food, toys, even custom-made collars. The woman keen to do that was forever chasing me for measurements, and I'd have these messages pinging through telling me how to measure a dog's neck while I was being shot and mortared at. The love shown to that little hairy bundle was definitely higher than the love shown to us big hairy men.

Later on I found out that Rocky was from a litter of seven that had been living in a nearby graveyard. Apparently someone had been keeping an eye on them, and noticed that a lot of the puppies had gone missing. I guess they went off to explore or to find food, and that is how Rocky had become trapped in the building. Well, he was safe now!

It sounds soft, but it was really nice to come back and find him waiting for us after a night on the front line. We had no wives to come home to, so Rocky was our cuddle at the end of a hard night's work dodging mortars. He'd have kept himself entertained in our absence chasing after the reams of plastic bottles lying around. The only bad thing he did was to bark relentlessly through the sunrise, which he hated for some reason. That was often the time we were getting back from the front and collapsing into bed, so it wasn't great. The boys could sleep through a mortar attack, but not Rocky's barking, and I'd hear some of them shouting out of their windows, 'Shut that fucking dog up, or I'm gonna have to shoot it!' and I'd be up like a shot, yelling: 'Don't touch him! He's a harmless puppy!' Pesh would treat the animals badly by Western standards but didn't dare touch them in front of us.

One afternoon during downtime I was working through the latest batch of Facebook messages I had received. I tried to get on social media once a day when we weren't too busy, as I saw it as a way of raising awareness of what we were doing.

It bothers me the amount of absolute idiots that want to come out and fight, though, or at least claim they do. 'Listen to these latest messages I have received,' I said to the room in general, where everyone was relaxing, cleaning weapons or on their phones. ' "I am planning to come out in four weeks, and am training hard for this on my video games. But am I best practising on *Call of Duty* or *Battlefield*, which one is closer to the situations I will be facing?"

'It's like, I really want to help people, and I know I relied heavily on a couple of people for info before I came, but seriously, are these people actually for real? OK, here's another. "I want to join the fight. I will be driving from South Carolina, can you tell me the best route? Also which state is Kurdistan in?" '

Everyone was sniggering as I kept reading out ridiculous message after ridiculous message. JP in particular was sat on the bed opposite, laughing his head off.

'Sorry, but I am beginning to think someone is taking the piss. Right, I'll read one more, then I'll stop. "My name is Sean, I have never been in the army or fired a weapon, nor been in a confrontational situation. I am however very good at track and field. When can I come and join you?"'

'I am genuinely disturbed that he could be heading our way to join us. I know I have read out the most extreme, but even the ones who ask questions like "what is the currency?" or "how hot is the temperature?" – do they not have Google?

'I know we're keen for people to join the fight, but I don't think we want anyone without basic initiative to come over. There are enough people here who are detrimental to the cause as it is.'

JP was nodding in agreement. He hadn't put himself out there so much on social media and wasn't doing any fundraising that way, but he said he was starting to get inundated with requests and mundane questions all the same.

'I need to add you on Facebook actually, mate, now you mention it,' I said. 'What's your Facebook name?'

Suddenly JP was no longer grinning but was glaring at me. 'I knew you never made the connection, you big fool! We are already Facebook friends, in fact we were long before I came out here. I asked for your help before I came, and you absolutely rubbered me!'

I laughed. 'You must have asked something bloody stupid then, and deserved it!'

Nevertheless JP's unhappy face told me he didn't agree, and I scrolled back through all my messages until I found him. It was true, I had ignored numerous reasonable questions from him, and when I decided he was hounding me had told him I was off out to dinner so we would have to talk later. Oops, I felt bad now. I tried to make up for it.

'Mate, you are mixed in amongst so many others,' I explained, 'I obviously just thought you were one of them.'

It seemed I had been so sick of the rubbish messages I had failed to notice when a good one came along.

We chatted about the difficulties we had faced getting info before we had come out, combined with the nuisance of inane messages now we were there. The more we talked, the clearer it became that there should be a source of information on the internet for anyone wanting to come and join the fight. At least if there was, it would stop us having to repeat for the three-hundredth time what kit is needed, no you can't bring weapons on the plane, what the weather is like, yes you can use American dollars out here, etc., etc.

Eventually I decided to make more of Improve the Situation than just a PayPal account to get funds. I decided to set it up as a source of information. I was already answering constant questions and keeping people posted on what was happening via my personal Facebook, but it made more sense to make it more official, and keep all the information in one place. So I set up the relevant Facebook page, bought a domain name (www.improvethesituation. co.uk) and got a friend at home to start designing it. Then I thought back to everything I had wanted to know before flying out, as well as the information I thought most people had asked me, and what was the most useful.

Most questions seemed to come under a set few areas – travel, i.e. getting there in the first place, the airports to go to, which taxis to use, visa requirements; kit, i.e. what to bring in terms of clothing and footwear, tactical equipment, weapons, medical supplies; money, i.e. what the currency is, how much to bring, what ATM and money exchange facilities there are; and politics, i.e. the current situation out there, in particular in the areas I was in, and if there are any cultural nuances that it's good for people to be aware of.

The new website seemed to be a useful tool, and I was able to refer people to that. It was also a good way for me to feel helpful, as I know I had needed that information before I came, and I was helping to prevent people making any daft mistakes. Who knows, something like my recommended kit list may have just stopped someone having an uncomfortable day of mosquito bites on the front line, or a piece of tactical equipment I suggested they bring could actually have saved a life.

7

THE DEFENCE OF
ST MATTHEW'S

During the conversations I had with the team while I was in Turkey, Gill mentioned something that sounded appealing. She told me: 'We've a possible upcoming job which will help us all out, give us freer rein, allow us to do what we came here for and take us away from the politics of Dwekh.'

It sounded good, but she was worried her phone was being monitored and said she would explain when I was back. So now that I was settled in Baqofa, and in the routine of the front line, I asked her about it.

'There is a monastery up in the mountains, not far from the front line, that was built two thousand years ago. It is called the Mor Mattai Monastery – or St Matthew's in English. Only a few people live and work there, and just a handful of Westerners have ever seen it. But as you know Daesh are destroying as many of these amazing historical sites as possible, and we are looking at getting the gig to secure it and stop anything happening there.'

She went on to explain that there was only one small road going up into the mountains to reach it, making it easier to secure. Although a Pesh detachment were looking after the area at the minute, it was the kind of place Daesh wouldn't expect to be guarded, so it was likely they would only send a small force up that we could deal with easily. Gill had been told the bishop was keen to improve on the security, and she suggested we go and see it and suss it out.

So we all bundled there one day in the truck, driving through the barren dusty plain then up the mountain to our destination, where we could see only rocks and small clumps of bushes for miles around. As we got towards the monastery two Pesh soldiers stepped forward, one in shorts, one in combat trousers with flip-flops. Gill wasn't wrong, it was obviously a very casual operation! A third came sauntering over holding an AK – the only guard with a weapon – but it was upside down and everything felt very relaxed. Through our translator they told us we couldn't come in, but Gill called the bishop, who gave us the permission to come ahead.

He met us in flowing black robes as we pulled up to the building, an incredible huge sand-coloured structure literally built into the cliff, with dozens of windows looking out over the view below.

The bishop told us he had worked as a physician in London years before, and lived in the Barbican there, then given all that up to move out here. He was a Coptic Christian, and he said this was supposed to have been a temporary posting, but he had never gone back to the UK.

He showed us around the place, which was breathtaking, and filled with all sorts of amazing artefacts – tapestries, the bones of saints, gold crosses and ancient relics. It felt like an incredibly special place that we were privileged to be allowed to see. He told us that over the years since it was built it had been repeatedly ransacked, and that a lot of crucial documents and historical artefacts had been destroyed. Despite this, there were a lot left, and it was particularly known for its library and collection of Syriac Christian manuscripts.

That the people fighting for Daesh could think a building with such a rich history as this was evil as opposed to incredibly special gave me more proof of how uneducated and uncivilized their leaders were. I felt a rush of repulsion that anyone would set out to destroy it.

But it seemed to us that coming on board to do the security was not going to be straightforward. Although the bishop was saying he was concerned about his current security, he told us that changing it in any way was a political issue and he wasn't sure anything could be done about it. 'Much as I would like you to, you can't get involved without it being sanctioned from the powers that be.'

There was also a French reporter with him who wouldn't explain why she was there, but was asking a lot about us, and whose presence put me on edge.

We left feeling a strange mix, awestruck at the actual

monastery, and a bit suspicious and disheartened, and I thought that was probably the end of it. Gill was particularly cut up about the negative vibe, as she felt it was her project, and she wasn't ready to give up yet.

It turned out that one of her contacts in Mosul, which had been occupied by Daesh since early 2014, had discussed the idea of starting to evacuate women and children from the city via the monastery, using it as a safe place for them before they could be moved on elsewhere. Its significance for Gill had become even higher.

At the time there seemed to be a constant stream of news emerging about the treatment of females, in particular those who were non-Muslim, by Daesh. There were reports of them being sold as sex slaves, repeatedly raped and beaten, forced into marriages and given as 'gifts', and not just the grown women, but girls, and even infants were reportedly being sold on. An apparent price list had even emerged months before, with the sickening figures showing that those aged one to nine years old were the most expensive. We were all exceptionally concerned by the reports, but Gill was particularly bothered by it, and talked about it frequently.

A few days later we were back in Duhok for a quick trip, and I had just dozed off, when at about 02:30 Gill came storming in: 'Right, the monastery's a goer! Get kitted up, get your stuff together and let's go there. It's all sorted.'

'Who has sanctioned it?' I mumbled from under my blanket.

'The bishop wants us there as the Pesh aren't doing what he needs and my contacts in the US say it is good for us to go there. So let's throw our stuff in bags and get there in taxis. We are going undercover.'

The others were awake by now, and JP spoke up: 'If this has not been sanctioned by Pesh it is not a goer, we are not doing it. We need the blessing of everyone. But you get Pesh to say it's fine, and I am there.'

Gill carried on as though she hadn't heard him. 'Right, we need a vehicle, and RPGs, more ammo . . .'

'Let's discuss it in the morning, Gill,' I said, agreeing with JP, my head full of sleep. Rolling over, I pulled the blanket back up. This was not something that needed deciding at 02:30!

The next day Gill presented me with a list of items that would be needed. She and Cory had drawn it up in the night, and was clear that as usual I was being asked to pay for it.

'If it is a hundred per cent a goer, I don't mind forking out but I am not wasting money on more shit.' I was referring to a previous time I had been talked into spending money on a load of gear that was still sat in the dungeon, unused.

Cory and I spent the day discussing vehicles with Iraqi second-hand-car salesmen, which was a tedious experience. The chat and the bullshit were even worse than you go through in the UK. We decided we liked a Toyota truck, but after arguments over a $250 difference, I couldn't take any more, and instead went with JP to see a chap called Blackjack. I wanted to buy 1,000 rounds of 7.62mm ammunition for the group, a figure that made sense if we might be digging in at the monastery for a while.

Blackjack was another local lad we'd bought weapons from previously. He owned a military store in town selling equipment, knives and general military and outdoor clothing, but away from the shop he had access to a lot more. I couldn't pronounce his real name, but he always wore a black jacket, hence the nickname.

He was good at getting hold of stuff, but very annoying in the way he drew out every meeting. It generally went like this: 'You are my brother, come to my shop and have chai, come and meet my family, you are my friend, drink water with me.'

'Blackjack, I just want a bag and some ammo, shut up, give me that and I'll be on my way!'

We had lots to get through that day, and I wasn't in the mood for one of Blackjack's drawn-out sessions. We got to his shop and he started to try and tell me about other items he was adamant that I wanted, but eventually he seemed to get it, and we agreed to meet that afternoon when he would have the rounds.

Once at his shop we had to wait for his brother to come and cover so Blackjack could leave, then he walked us across town to a deserted car park. It was a big open space hidden from view by a few houses, with no one else around, and something about it didn't feel quite right. I was just in shorts and flip-flops, as I hadn't thought it was the time for full-on tactical gear, but a bit of me was aware how vulnerable we were.

Blackjack's contact arrived and began fiddling around in the back of the car, while Blackjack chatted on and on, not actually saying anything, just mindlessly babbling.

'What's the problem? I have the money, can we get what we came for, please?' I pushed.

'You're my friend, I do this for you,' he told me. 'Maybe you want some other stuff at the same time.'

Then he and his contact began arguing between themselves in Kurdish, with things getting animated. We had no clue what was being said, or what was going on. Then a third guy appeared from behind the houses, walking over to us.

'Fucking hell, who's this?' said JP, turning to keep a close eye on him.

I was on edge, and unhappy with the situation. Every bit of me felt this set-up wasn't right, and that we were at a disadvantage. I didn't need to be a trained soldier to know this – my days in the prison and on doors meant I trusted my gut to know when something was a bit odd. I also knew the longer we stayed, the more any risk escalated.

Blackjack started trying to chat to me again, suggesting all sorts of extra weapons and equipment I could buy, and I felt sure he was delaying for some reason, so I cut him short.

'We do it as I said, or it doesn't happen at all. If you

have the thousand rounds I will take them, if not, forget it.'

'Easy mate, don't blow,' JP warned me, putting his hand on my arm. But I was sure something was wrong, and the two men began arguing between themselves again.

'Right, you can stick it, I am out of here,' I said and I turned and walked away.

JP turned to Blackjack: 'I don't know what game you are playing, or if you are turning this into something it isn't, but we don't want this bullshit, end of.' He followed me out of the car park.

I was wound up and on edge, and it was a relief to get back to the house. It is not always easy interpreting body language and inflection, even when you are in your own country, culture, and speaking your own language. So at times in Kurdistan it felt nigh on impossible to read people's intentions, feelings and motives. For example, the Kurds are much more animated in conversation and raise their voice much more readily than Brits. What seems like a heated exchange between two men that looks ready to spill over into physical violence might be something as simple as a small tiff over who should go and get the water bottles today. Over time I got used to it, but it was still harder to predict people than back home.

As it transpired, Blackjack turned up at the house that night with the thousand rounds I had asked for. 'You are my brother,' he told me. 'I don't want to argue.'

'We have no problems between us, Blackjack,' I said, 'but for once, please shut the fuck up!'

I hoped he was telling the truth, as I wanted to have faith in everyone I had dealings with out there. But I know from experience to trust my instincts, and was sure there had been something more to the day's events than met the eye. I would be even more cautious in any future dealings with Blackjack.

Tex had been out looking at weapons for the monastery job, and had got someone to visit the house with a whole range of RPGs and grenades. The guy's bag was full and, like a kid in a sweet shop, Tex told me he wanted it all. Knowing just how much that would cost, I started choosing some to stay and some to go. Tex got a bit sulky.

'I want it all.'

'We don't need it all. If you want it, you can pay for it.'

The idea that I was endlessly bankrolling the missions out there was getting a bit wearing. Although to be fair to Tex, he was the only person out of everyone I bought a rifle for who paid me back, and without being asked.

That evening I pulled JP aside. 'What's your view on this mission?'

'Honestly, I'm not keen. It's a pie in the sky dream, that if it hasn't been sanctioned will see us run out of the country, or something go majorly wrong. We will be completely isolated out there with no back-up, and great, we think they won't send many guys, but what if they send a hundred? We would be fucked. It is not a sensible thing to do, especially if we don't know that we have the Peshmerga onside. We are getting to the front here each day, I'd like to stick that out instead, and see if we can't increase our efforts here.'

I completely agreed with him, and added: 'At the end of the day, the Peshmerga aren't interested in saving old buildings. It's not what's important to them, and understandably they would rather save people's lives. I am happy to go up against Daesh on that mountain, and if we can help the people needing to escape Mosul it would be amazing. But only if it is through the channels of the people who have given us our passes to be here in the first place.'

It was good to know that JP and I were on the same wavelength. I hadn't known the guy that long, but I trusted his judgement, so when we both had a bad feeling about something, I was sure we were right about it. I called a meeting.

'Gill, I am going to be straight with you. This is where I stand. I am not up for this. You always have these clandestine calls with your contacts that we aren't involved in, and I am not sure we know everything about this project. If you want to get it set up, go for it, I know it means a lot to you. We are only half an hour away, so if anything goes wrong you know we will do our best to help.'

JP said: 'I'm with Tim. I want to give the front line a good go down here, and not throw all that away. Good luck to you all, though.'

The three others accepted what we said, but were clearly disappointed. Gill turned to Cory and Tex, who said they still wanted to go. Jimbo wasn't planning to go either, so we divided our stuff, and the Americans left for the monastery, and the Brits went back to the house at the front line.

8

RAMADAN

Back on the front line things were moving up a gear. The holy month of Ramadan began on 18 June and with it the number of attacks escalated instantly. While I had been consistent in my belief that this was not a holy war from our end, the increase proved that as far as Daesh were concerned religion was the excuse they were hiding behind for their actions. Talking to soldiers who had fought in Iraq and Afghanistan, I learned this escalation of attacks by extremists during Ramadan is to be expected, and in fact at this time Daesh put out a call to their supporters to step up assaults on a worldwide scale.

The mortar attacks, which had been mainly taking place at night, became much more frequent in the day too, so that mortar rounds seemed to be dropping constantly in Baqofa. They caused damage everywhere they landed, and as a result they were more frequently on target. Whereas mortar fire had been aimed at the front line, during Ramadan it was much more constant in reaching back into the village and nearer to the houses. It was common to wake up to the dull thud of a mortar hitting the ground, followed by the bouncing and shattering of splash – everything that flies out from the mortar's point of impact such as shrapnel and rocks. Quite a few buildings were hit, including a couple of the guard posts and houses in the village. The forward operating base was clearly a target, but luckily while mortars repeatedly landed in the courtyard and ground around it, the building itself never took a direct hit. Not that this meant there was no damage to the buildings. Splash can be very damaging too. Due to the number of shots on target we increased the structural security at our three houses. We spent a day with bulldozers moving dirt up against the buildings, compacting it in against the walls.

I often found it more frustrating than frightening to be at the front on these occasions, however, as it was rare that we were allowed to return fire. It was constantly reiterated to us by Ahmed and Pesh officials that 'We are here to hold the front line, not to attack' and that retaliation was only when necessary. They also saw it as a waste of ammunition and would point out how expensive mortar rounds were.

In terms of human casualties, the upside of so many of the homes in the village remaining empty was that hardly anyone was inside when they were struck, so civilian casualties were prevented. Occasionally though, a Pesh soldier would be hit, and there were some pretty bad injuries to legs and arms. These were often caused by the splash, as burning-hot pieces of shrapnel shred flesh, so it was always a case of getting them to the medical centre as quickly as possible. Often the soldiers would be proud of their injuries. I suppose they were a sign that they had survived an attack, and despite what Daesh had fired at them they were still standing. They would show off their scars at any opportunity, keen to retell the tale of their survival.

With the Peshmerga a predominantly Muslim army, it was interesting to watch how their soldiers behaved during Ramadan, compared with the reports we were getting about the Daesh fighters. For me, it summed up the hypocrisy of the enemy. It seemed that the majority of Daesh fighters had made the decision that as they were fighting jihad – holy war – it was not necessary to fast. Their argument was apparently that they needed their energy reserves to be at a maximum. For people who claim to be so ultra-devout, I felt as though they were using the battle as a 'get out of jail free' card – a cop-out from the fast that they were so insistent everyone else follow.

In fact, in those first weeks of Ramadan reports came through of some young boys in Syria who, struggling to cope with fasting in the heat, had caved in and made themselves a small meal. When Daesh discovered this, they crucified the boys as an example to anyone else who might give in to the temptation of food or drink. From men who were using a loophole to feed themselves, I found this a horrific story of hypocrisy and inhumane behaviour that needed to be stamped out at all costs.

Meantime the guys in the Peshmerga followed their faith to the letter. They would not eat between sunrise and sunset, or drink anything. Given that the temperature could rise to 48 degrees in the day, to turn down even a sip of water was incredible dedication. And still they did their jobs properly. There was no calling in sick, crying off from heat exhaustion or asking for a lie-in. I'll be honest, they would look like shit by the end of every day, but they really did stick to it.

I felt guilty one morning when a Peshmerga friend came to visit the house and I was there, not only cooking myself a big fry-up, but one containing bacon no less. I'd even offered him a drink before I realized what a bad friend I was being!

Their dedication to their religion, combined with their determination to keep defending their people against these zealots during Ramadan, was particularly impressive and heartening to see.

Although the General was back and around next door, we still hadn't had a chance to properly meet him, something JP and I were desperate to do as we felt sure he would get us better access to the fighting. Early one morning while I was in bed asleep, JP was on the roof doing stag when the General came out of his house and shouted to JP to come and meet him. JP ran down, and the General signalled for him to get in his truck. They went off to the front line together where JP spent the next few hours firing off mortar rounds and dealing with incoming, while Marcus translated anything the General wished to say. At one point the General told him: 'We have had a big problem with people filming and putting it on the internet. Yes, others are interested to see it but it is also helping Daesh know where mortar rounds are coming from, and specific details of our defences. As you know they are close enough to see details of our building and terrain, so they can match this up with the footage and I believe that is why some of the mortar rounds have been so accurate lately. So now I say, if anyone films things they shouldn't, I will chop their hands off.' It was something we had always been aware of – not giving away details that could compromise anything in our social media posts – but with the General's warning, we were even more careful from then on. We were sure this was a man whose threats were not to be taken lightly.

That morning JP watched as the General bravely crossed into no-man's-land to disarm an IED planted by Daesh. He wouldn't let any of his troops come with him as he didn't want to put them in danger. He dealt with it himself and it was clear he was a man who led by example.

I was furious when JP came back to the house and told me all of this. Why hadn't he woken me? I would have been up and out of there in seconds given the opportunity to spend a few hours on the front with the General!

Luckily I didn't have to wait long for my own taste of it as just that evening Ahmed came charging into the house shouting to us to get our kit as we were heading out. As usual with Ahmed the details were scarce, so not knowing what kit we would need, I grabbed just about everything, and loaded myself up.

My typical choice of gear for trips to the front line was head to toe MP, knee pads and Meindl desert boots, and sunglasses, depending on the time of day and weather. I'd take my AK, a high-leg holster with my pistol, and my rig, which had eight magazines of AK ammunition, six mags for my Glock, and a paddle with twelve shotgun shells in it. Smaller bits such as handcuffs would go in my admin pouch, while my wallet and passport, which I took with me everywhere, were tucked inside a zipped section of my Osprey meant for soft body armour.

All kitted out, JP, Jimbo and I all charged down the stairs and onto the road at the back of the houses with the rest of the Dwekh boys to join the Pesh who were already there, kitted up and getting into vehicles. The General was screaming and shouting so loudly I am sure Daesh themselves heard his instructions. Let's just say my first impressions were that he was definitely not a quiet, un-assuming man.

The problem for us at times like this was that every-thing was spoken in Kurdish or Assyrian. I had picked up the odd word, like *mumkin*, which means 'maybe' – a response that seemed to me to be given in answer to

everything – but that was about the extent of my understanding. Now the few locals who spoke good English and
would translate for us were too busy getting themselves
organized and obeying instructions to help us, so we clambered into the trucks along with everyone else, just hoping
we were doing the correct thing.

The truck took us the seven hundred metres to the
front line. It might seem ridiculous to drive such a short
distance, but with all the gear everyone was carrying it
seemed the easiest way.

The section of the front line that we looked after was
about two kilometres long. Every two hundred and fifty
metres or so there was a guard station, where a rotation
of Peshmerga soldiers ate, slept and observed. We pulled
up to the first of these and everyone bundled out. We were
signalled to go inside along with the General, and the rest
of the guys filed in behind us – about forty people trying
to fit into this one small room. The soldiers stationed there
stood up, and there was much handshaking and talking. The General was asking questions of the soldiers, and
giving them what from his tone and body language I
deduced were words of encouragement. I studied him, and
decided he must be about forty years old, and despite not
being very tall – maybe around five foot nine – he held
himself in an imposing way. His chest was constantly
puffed out, and he held his back ramrod-straight. He gave
off the air of a man who believed in himself, would be fair
to others, but wouldn't suffer fools gladly.

We were given chai and watermelon, and people asked

to look at our rifles, while the General sat next to us, chain-smoking Marlboro cigarettes and watching. The Peshmerga soldiers were supplied with their weapons upon joining, and often found themselves with old rifles from previous wars that had pieces missing or were beginning to rust. The soldiers didn't tend to spend their own money on improving them, and on the whole we had taken better care of our weapons, so they were keen to inspect our handiwork. The pistols, which are carried by very few people out there, also caused much interest. The guys kept pointing in amazement to the fact I was carrying twelve magazines and a big pouch of shotgun shells. They never carried more than three magazines at a time, but I was determined not to be caught short, and besides, I still had no idea what we were aiming to do that evening.

The men said thank you to us a lot, and patted us on the back, but beyond that we couldn't follow the conversation and had no idea what was being discussed. Then suddenly everyone was out of their seats, and we were up and off out of there. The General waved us over to his truck, a Toyota Hilux, and JP jumped into the passenger seat. Between my bulk and everything I was carrying, I couldn't physically get in the front of a truck like this without squashing the driver into his window, so I jumped into the back flatbed, along with two of the General's bodyguards who called themselves Special Forces. Indeed one of my first taxi drivers in the country had told me, 'I am also a fighter. I am a soldier with the Peshmerga, and am Special Forces.' I had been so impressed, but after I heard it time and again, I learned that practically everyone in Iraq who gets to hold a gun as part of their job refers to themselves as Special Forces. It doesn't quite come with the prestige out there that it does in the UK!

I sat on the side of the truck, relaxing as I had done on our journeys in the Dwekhmobile, but the bodyguards signalled frantically for me to get down into the truck bed and hold on to the sides, and suddenly without warning we were off. Let's just say this wasn't one of those comfy trips in the Dwekhmobile, with its soft seats and smooth travel. Someone's rifle was sticking in my ribs, a box of grenades was bouncing under my feet and as we jolted over every bump it felt like if I didn't break my back then at the very least I'd be thrown out of the vehicle. Half the flatbed was taken up by a large storage box, so it was an even tighter squeeze than normal.

We were travelling at about 65 kph, flying over rough ground, uneven and full of rocks. I made sure to keep tight hold of my weapon, as even though it was attached to my body armour with a single-point sling, I didn't feel in total control of it.

After a few minutes the truck stopped and we fell out.

'That was quite a ride!' said a laughing JP, slapping me on the shoulder.

'Mate, you had a seatbelt,' I replied breathlessly. 'You have no idea . . .'

We were now at the next guard post along, and going in I tried to stand at the back of the crowd. I like to have my back against the wall to see what's going on. I think that is a habit that was drilled into me in my days as a prison guard, when you would never have a prisoner behind you but would always make sure they were in your field of vision. It doesn't mean I didn't trust the guys I was with, it's just instinctive to make sure I have everything and everyone in sight when possible. I am the same if I go to a restaurant, I like to be on a table by the wall, and I need to be sat in the seat facing outwards, to keep an eye on everything happening within the vicinity. I don't think the rest of the diners are about to attack me, but I have learnt to feel safest that way, so if I want to be relaxed, it is necessary.

But once again JP and I were pushed forward, this time to sit with the General, while everyone else stood around. I was afraid to sit down, as the seats looked like those white plastic garden chairs that fall apart when you set a lettuce leaf on them. I weigh 110 kilos normally, and 150 kilos with all my equipment on, so was genuinely concerned I would be through it and onto the floor before I knew it. JP doesn't weigh much less and cheekily waited for me to sit first, giving a sideways glance and winding me up: 'The legs are going, mate,' before he sat down himself.

This time coffee and water came out with the slices of watermelon, and the chat continued in Kurdish, at times soft-spoken and relaxed, at other times descending to shouting. I looked around for Marcus or one of the other boys who could translate, but they were stuck at the back of the group.

JP grinned at me and shrugged. We clearly both had the same thought – that we had no idea what the hell was going on, but it was an experience, so we would just go with the flow!

One thing we could tell though, without speaking the language, was just how much energy and enthusiasm oozed out of the General. It was clear that not only did everyone respect him, but they were getting fired up in his presence. It was remarkable to see the effect he had on these soldiers, some of whom had looked tired and dejected when we arrived. They did long hours at their posts, which could be quiet and mind-numbing one minute and life-threatening the next. While I already respected him, I found myself growing more in awe of him too.

Again at this stop-off soldiers were poking at my weapons and equipment and taking things out to look at without asking permission. I didn't like it, but some of them were pretty senior officers so I wasn't going to argue with them. This lack of boundaries with belongings was their culture, and I had to accept that.

This same pattern was repeated in several more lookout points, until I couldn't take any more offers of drink or food. So when the next tray of watermelons arrived, I went to pass it on to the standing men without taking any.

'No, no!' I was told. 'For you.'

'I've had enough, maybe they want some?'

'No, only for you!'

I called Marcus to come and help me, and said: 'Can you please explain that the other people here are on exactly the same night mission as we are, and as such they will need sustenance. Please can we share it around? This is getting embarrassing and I don't want to feel like we are being treated differently.'

Marcus translated nervously, and the General studied me for a few moments, his face giving very little away. Then he waved for it to go around, but the Pesh were actually not happy to get the food. They ate it, but almost as though under duress, because for them it wasn't the norm and they felt awkward. Originally thinking I was doing them a favour I began to wish I'd kept my mouth shut.

A little later we were heading back to the vehicles to drive on, when Marcus called us back: 'This way!' The General had headed to the berm instead and run over the top of it and onto the flat piece of land beyond, followed closely by his bodyguards. I watched confused, but Marcus followed, and then JP, who yelled: 'Big T! Get your arse over here!' as he disappeared over the top.

I glanced around for Jimbo, but couldn't see him. So head down, I ran over the berm too. I was now on a flat piece of land, twenty metres wide, between the berm and the defensive trench, which ran from west to east. The berm is the official front line, so for some reason we were now in front of it. Without the berm, we had no protection from Daesh shooting at us, and at this range a mortar or Dushka round could hit us no problem.

We set off along this line at quite a speed, fast-marching alongside the trench. It was awful terrain and I was stumbling all the time, tripping on rubbish, sandbags, and piles of dirt that I couldn't see in the darkness until it was too late. Every thirty metres or so we would pause, while there was a lot of shouting into the desert. I couldn't understand what was being shouted, but we were told that the thermal scope had picked up on people running around in this no-man's-land, and assuming it was Daesh, the idea was to intimidate them. There was nothing between us and them, and in the desert sound travels better at night, especially as it was so still, so forty voices all yelling actually did sound pretty threatening. We joined in, shouting our own obscenities in English, guessing at the kind of things they might be saying in Kurdish. 'You big hairy ball sacks!' screamed JP, then ducking ran on. As the insults we shouted became more and more ridiculous, it added a comical side to what was actually a very dangerous position. Sometimes the guys would fire off their weapons too. If they saw the slightest movement or heard a little noise, they would open up like crazy people into the darkness. When I shoot, it is a controlled burst of two or three rounds. They think nothing of firing off thirty rounds in one go, and without even looking down the sight. They will just fire in the general direction until their magazine empties.

We were in a rough line formation, with JP and me at the back. This had happened partly because we were carrying so much more equipment, and with the heat and the weight, we were a bit slower, but it was out of choice too. These boys were so trigger-happy, the last thing I wanted was to be in front of them when they let off a hail of bullets without thinking about which way they were going. I'll be honest, I didn't give up my life at home and come here to get shot in the back by an overenthusiastic local. Life over here is very cheap too, so they would be upset at the time, don't get me wrong, but by the next day it would be, 'Oh dear, I shot one of the Western volunteers' and the day after that they would have forgotten about me.

Suddenly the shouting stopped, and the General sat down on the ground. Everyone else joined him, despite the fact we were in an extremely vulnerable position. I looked at JP, who shrugged, 'When in Rome,' and sat down.

Everyone was chatting amongst themselves and soldiers kept scampering over to sit between us, asking for photos and wanting to play with our gear. Suddenly a little guy came running down the berm behind me carrying a cool box. He opened it up and started pulling out little bottles of cold water. Most of the Western volunteers carry Camelbaks – I had one that carried three litres – but I was still happy to accept a fresh one after all the buckets I had sweated in the last couple of hours.

Behind this guy came another man carrying a silver tray on which were balanced little glasses of chai on saucers. He handed me one along with a couple of lumps of sugar. I had no idea where these self-appointed waiters came from, but guessed they were soldiers from a guard post just out of view over the berm.

'What's going on here?' I said to JP. 'We're in the middle of the front line dealing with a possible attack, and we're

140

sitting drinking chai. Not only that, but we're sat completely unprotected, out in the open?'

'Never in my life . . .' Then he shook his head – that was about as much as he could manage!

'Seriously, though,' I persevered. 'I don't get it. This is not how we should do it. We need to be quiet, set up an ambush, let them come to us, and then we kill them.'

'Tim, mate, we are here to do as they tell us. If this is how they want to play it, we just have to go with it.'

I guess that was the difference between me and someone who had been in the army, and knew better than I did how to obey orders without question.

Just then there was a nudge at my shoulder, and I kid you not, the next guy was there, holding a big silver bowl of mixed nuts.

'No, I'm OK, thanks.'

'Take some,' he said emphatically, pushing the bowl right under my nose. Then I remembered that while back home it is culturally no problem to refuse something, in the Middle East they often see it as an insult. At times I found this attitude came across as very pushy, but it was because they would worry they weren't feeding you enough, and so felt happier if you accepted. I took a small handful of pistachios. That was apparently not good enough, as the guy grabbed my hands and tipped half the bowl into them, so that I was overflowing with what felt like a good half-kilo of nuts. I tried to tip them all into one hand, losing plenty onto the sand in the process, and took my hat off to put the remainder in there. JP was rolling around laughing – until the guy headed over to him.

As I sat back munching, the General started telling stories, and this time Marcus translated for us.

'I want to push ahead and do more, attack more villages,' he said, 'but I have been told by Barzani that this is not an option at the moment. We must wait and hold the line tight here until he allows us to push on further.

'I have killed many men, and am very committed to this cause. I have lost three brothers to the fight and I want to get revenge for them, and all the other people who have suffered at the hands of Daesh. I like to cut the ears of dead Daesh and keep them as a memento.'

JP and I exchanged glances. 'Er, could you get him to expand on the last bit, please?' we said to Marcus.

Obligingly, he continued. 'I give you an example. One day we went to a village to clear it of Daesh. In one house I found a couple of the rats still hiding there. One tried to attack me and we fought in hand-to-hand combat. I won, and stabbed him in the chest. I decided I needed to take his ears, so I started cutting them off. He was still alive. One of my soldiers came in and went to shoot him, but I told him: "Leave him, he will die of his own accord." They are nothing these people, they are not humans, so I have no feelings for them except hatred.'

We sat quietly for a bit then, and I was thinking about what he said. Even before I was out in Kurdistan I knew I would have no problem shooting a member of Daesh, and I have no issue with them dying, but to go to those lengths to increase their suffering . . . It was not for me, but at the same time I felt as though I could understand why he would do it. The pain they had put him through, particularly by killing three of his brothers; I could see that this was his way of dealing with it. It wasn't for me to judge his behaviour, or that of any of the Peshmerga soldiers for that matter. Their lives had been impacted by the existence of Daesh in a way that it was impossible to understand without having lived through it.

By now my mouth was so dry from all the nuts I could hardly speak, and I was beginning to feel a bit unwell. I had somehow managed to drink all of the water provided, plus my own supply and couldn't possibly eat any more, so I tried to discreetly dig a hole in the ground and bury the remaining nuts there. I felt quite dizzy and sick, and was only half-joking when I said to JP: 'Do you think there is any way to do the same thing with some of the magazines? Bury them here and come back for them in the morning, to lessen my load!'

But before I knew it, with no warning we were up and off again. The ground was so rough at this point that walking across the dirt was like trying to cross a ploughed field. I was puffing and panting, and while part of me was enjoying the night, the other half was wondering if it would ever end. I generally consider myself to be pretty fit, so wasn't happy to feel I was struggling more than the others.

We carried on visiting more guard posts, and it was clear the General loved having two massive Brits running alongside him in all their gear. Each place we stopped he would find a new piece of our equipment to show off. He particularly liked JP's state-of-the-art night-vision goggles and the laser attachment on my rifle. It was a powerful tool, and would go as far as you could see, cutting straight through the darkness, and fantastic at picking out targets.

Finally we reached the end of our section of the front line, and standing in the open waiting for our next instructions, I dropped to one knee taking a defensive pose. If there was a sniper out there, the man standing would be the easiest target, so would be the one hit. It seemed at times as though JP and I were the only ones aware of the enemy out there, as all the Pesh stood around without a care in the world. Perhaps I thought about it more as it was all new to me. For them, this daily battle was a way of life, and no one can live their lives in a constant state of high alert. They had developed an acceptance of it, I suppose.

I had a bigger concern than any sniper, though – as I knelt there puffing and panting I was aware that the whole route had been ever so slightly downhill, which meant only one thing. It was going to be more hellish on the return.

The General headed up the berm to sit on the sandbags at the top, surrounded by the various commanders, laughing and smoking. I realized how smart he was being. He had done a great job of motivating all these guys who a few hours before were thoroughly fed up of manning these posts, dealing with incoming mortar rounds day after day, but with no chance of advancing. Let's face it, a lot of the time their days were pretty boring, waiting for action. But the General had apparently just received intel that there was something going on in the Daesh camp, and as such it was a good evening to make sure everyone was ready for any action. And it had worked. He had made sure that everyone at the posts were doing their jobs properly and looking after themselves, for example that they were sleeping undercover to avoid shrapnel, and were getting fed well enough. Now they were re-energized, motivated, and keen to do anything their boss told them to. He was the top guy, and you felt you had to be at the top of your game for him.

By now I was getting sick of the photos the locals kept taking on their phones. Not only did it obviously alert the enemy to exactly where we were, but it totally killed night vision. Each time my eyes had begun adjusting to the darkness, a flash would go off and I'd be blinded again for a few minutes. But it was like everyone was actually enjoying this outing and keen to keep a record of it.

I sighed with relief a few minutes later when the trucks arrived to pick us up. It seemed the General had decided a walk in just one direction was enough. It was the usual run and dive to get into the back before we were off. Normally once everyone was in and comfortable, one of the guys in the back would tap the side of the truck to let the driver know they could set off. But no one would do that to the General's vehicle, partly because banging would seem almost disrespectful, but quite frankly they were also shit-scared of him.

We retraced our steps, this time in a vehicle and on the defensive side of the berm, and stopped at any guard point we had missed on the way down. I think there were about eight in total. At 02:00 we finally got to the last one, and found Jimbo there along with Ramen and a couple of other Dwekh lads. He laughed at me, covered in dirt and dust, with the sweat lashing off me.

I looked around this stop-off, which was by a four-metre gap in the berm where the road used to run between the villages of Baqofa and Batnaya. The Pesh had parked up a big American Humvee. They told me they had taken it from Iraqi troops who had been fleeing from Daesh. The Pesh had stopped them at a checkpoint, and when they realized they were escaping rather than fighting, dragged them out of the vehicle and told them to go and get a cab instead. Understandably the Pesh soldiers standing their ground had no respect for those who had decided they had had enough. So they sent them on their way and kept the Humvee.

They gave us a tour of the vehicle, and it was impressive stuff. A huge four-seater, it had thermal imaging that was controlled by two guys sat in the back. One of them had the remotes and would be zooming in and out while the other looked at the monitor. The General took over the monitor and shouted instructions as he searched for any sign of movement from Daesh. The whole thing probably cost around three or four million pounds, and was easily their best bit of kit. It was very striking that the people who were really fighting this war for the rest of the world were not the ones who were getting the financial aid from abroad. That had gone to the Iraqi army, which had fled when the going got tough, while these guys who had stood their ground were getting nothing. It seemed both ironic and unfair.

I went and sat on a bank of earth needing five minutes' rest. I was feeling really quite sick now, and physically and mentally fucked. I knew I was strong, but I started worrying that maybe my fitness levels weren't up to scratch and if we were doing this every night I would be in serious trouble.

The General began shouting instructions, and we headed across the twenty metres in front of the berm to the trench dividing us from no-man's-land. A guy appeared with a steel ladder which he laid across the trench. It just about reached, lying on the mud at both ends. I am guessing this is the Daesh ladder – so-called because it was stolen from them during a raid – and JP had told me this is what the General had used the night before to cross the trench to disarm the mines.

The General strode onto the ladder, stepping across each rung confidently, as though it was a normal footpath. We were less convinced, knowing that just because the nimble little locals had got across, it didn't mean the dirt at the sides of the trench would hold our weight on the ladder, despite being baked in the sun for the last six months.

Once over, the General and a couple of his men started scouting for mines, and we were told to cover them. We dropped to one knee and scanned the area for any sign of movement. Ahmed, who had been hovering in the background throughout the whole evening, stayed with us. Out of the corner of my eye I saw him watching me and JP and when he thought we weren't looking, he would readjust himself to copy JP, everything from his stance to turning his cap backwards. It was funny viewing, but I had another flash of irritation that this guy had so much sway over our daily activities.

There were a few explosions out ahead where mines had been found, and once again the General had taken it upon himself to disarm them with controlled explosions. Then the guys all started heading back. I realized looking around that I was making out a bit more of the world. The sun was just starting to rise – the time when an attack was most likely. I lay down on the berm and set myself up, thinking: 'Please let this be the time.' Just as I went off into a reverie of single-handedly taking down several members of Daesh, I got a kick in the ribs.

It was JP. 'What are you doing?'

Suddenly I felt a bit silly, lying there while they all packed up the truck, and slowly I stood up and joined them to head back. I could hardly walk now I was so tired, and I felt even sicker and almost delirious. I consoled myself by thinking of the bed waiting for me. I no longer cared that the room was smelly and messy, and even at this time of day would be roasting hot.

'The General has invited us all in for breakfast,' Marcus said to me. I groaned. I had wanted nothing more than to get to know the General better, but now I wasn't sure I would survive it. 'Please send my apologies,' I said, 'but I am ill. Don't let him be offended, but I really need to get my head down.'

I headed for bed and slept solidly for about seven hours, but getting up I felt even worse and started being sick. I left the front line and got a taxi back to town, thinking a day or two in Duhok might allow me a better chance of recovery. But when the sickness was becoming even more frequent on the Sunday, I got a cab to Erbil and checked myself in to the Life Support Team medical centre, a private hospital that deals with everything from supplying ambulances to the front line to dentistry. It turned out I had food poisoning. So I spent three days there with a drip in my arm while I slowly stopped being ill and regained some strength. When I left and had to pay my bill, it turned out to be less than $100 for the whole thing. While they may not have the NHS out there, that was a great price, for actually, pretty decent treatment. Buying any other medication I needed was equally cheap and easy, although the system definitely has the potential to be abused – you don't need a prescription but just buy medication for pennies. I'm not actually sure how the country isn't full of addicts. It was ironic though, as I had thought prescription drugs would be difficult to get, and had asked people in the UK to get me antibiotics, etc. before I left thinking I should have them on me. What a waste of money.

The night after I left the medical centre I checked into a hotel to give myself twenty-four hours to get my strength back before heading back to the front line. While I was there I weighed myself and was shocked to see I was down to 98 kilos. In the three days I was sick I had lost 12 kilos. I wasn't happy about it, but I know plenty of people who wouldn't mind going on such a fast-working diet!

9

BACK IN BAQOFA

Back in Baqofa the boys were pleased to see me, and it felt good to be back, even if I did come in for my fair share of mick-taking. The only food I could think of to blame for making me sick was a falafel I had got from a food shack we often visited. The guy who ran it was great and really friendly and the food made a good change from the usual, so I was gutted that he had poisoned me . . . unintentionally or not! When I got back to Baqofa, the Dwekh boys had drawn a picture on the wall of a falafel with eyes, holding a gun and shooting me. It said 'Big T, felled by a falafel' and they had a field day with the jokes. I'd gone all the way to Iraq to get involved in the war, only to be taken down by the food rather than the Daesh mortars. Of course I was always offered falafel when we went out for dinner too, but even to this day the sight of it instantly makes me feel sick.

The boys had looked after Rocky well while I was

gone, too well if I am honest, as he seemed to have tripled in size. Who knows what they were feeding him, but it was great when he ran over to see me on my return, and was really excited.

Another positive was that JP had cleared out a spare room which had been used to store a load of old junk. He got rid of it all and moved our beds in there so we could escape the smell of the communal bedroom, and everyone could spread out a bit more. He found an air-con unit in one of the other abandoned houses and, drilling holes in the wall, installed it to try and combat the intense heat. Ironically it worked so well we were now sometimes too cold and didn't want to get out of our sleeping bags in the morning. But ultimately the whole move did make the living arrangements that bit more bearable.

The other thing that had happened in my absence was the return of Tex. The full story of what happened at the monastery was a bit blurry, but Tex told us that he, Gill and Cory had started to investigate the area around the site, including the hill it was built on, so they could be as prepared as possible for any attack. Loads of tunnels and tombs have been cut into the hillside around the monastery, and when they began looking into them the bishop started getting jumpy, to the point that the team began to wonder if there was something hidden there. They also began to talk to the bishop about the idea of setting up an escape route for people in Mosul that went via the monastery, but apparently he was dead set against it. Tex said Gill was really upset by this, as she thought he would have

Top At Baqofa near our FOB. From left to right: Jimbo, me, Ramen, JP and Marcus. *Above* Tex back in the house at Duhok. He's a quirky comical genius – I love the guy. *Left* On the front line near Baqofa, looking across to the Daesh-occupied village of Batnaya on the horizon.

Meeting General Kovle (on the far right) at his base in Duhok. The General is an impressive man, forward-thinking, fearless and dedicated.

On General Kovle's orders, we were sitting on the wrong side of the berm, with no protection against Daesh if they decided to shoot at us. The General, meanwhile, was telling us stories. It was all about boosting the morale of the Peshmerga soldiers – but I did feel exposed!

Rocky, the puppy I found in
an abandoned courtyard.

With Gill and Tex on our trip to
the Mor Mattai monastery.

As seen through
JP's night-vision goggles.

Some members of IDET with the Hummer after the IED hit.

On the Peshmerga base.

The room I shared with three other guys at IDET.

Soaking up the sun on a brief break while waiting for our orders.
We were going to provide cover for some special-forces guys.

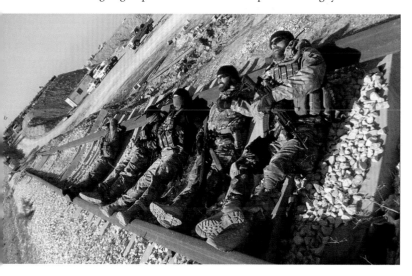

Top Christmas Eve saw us clearing a village after an airstrike. We found evidence that Daesh had been camping out. *Above left* Holding the back end of a smart bomb which the Lieutenant wanted me to carry back. *Above right* JP holding our Christmas lunch! Yellow shit and bread.

Carrying 'the Egyptian', along with everything else.

With JP on lookout.

Supermarket shopping, Kirkuk style.

With another member of IDET on the front line in January 2016.

Taking the armoured personnel carrier out for a spin.

been keen to help those trying to escape Mosul, especially as so many of them were Christians. It wasn't a problem she had predicted in her plans, but his main focus seemed to be more about protecting the monastery itself.

The few Pesh guys we had met on our visit were still up there, and there was a large base nearby. One day a general appeared, and told the Americans: 'You guys are moving out. I have found a house for you down by our base, so you are moving there.'

Tex knew something wasn't quite right, and figured it had become a case of them sticking their noses in too much and causing too much of a stir.

'I'd like to go back to Baqofa to my original unit, please,' he told the General, who jumped on this idea, and much to Tex's relief put him straight into a taxi back to us.

We got the rest of the story on text from Cory and Gill, who felt they had no choice but to move to the new house. They had only stayed there for one night, when the General appeared and said: 'You guys are going to Erbil, and I want you out of the country by the end of the week.'

The two of them were terrified they were going to end up in prison, or worse, and didn't know what the hell was happening. They got to Erbil and sold all their equipment and bought plane tickets to Paris. After that Cory went on to the States and Gill headed for Israel. She had some concerns about returning since Israeli citizens are actually forbidden from entering Iraq as their government deems it to be an enemy country, but she got home safely.

I was sad to see it hadn't worked out for them at the monastery, but glad that JP and I had trusted our instincts. Something hadn't felt right about it, and even though we will probably never know exactly what – if anything – was going on up there it had seemed clear from our initial visit that they didn't want our help.

I have a lot of time for Gill, but I was never sure who half her contacts were, and they may or may not have been giving her reliable information. She's a strong girl though whose heart is in the right place, and her departure wasn't the end of her involvement in the war. She has since gone on to do some great work campaigning to raise awareness of the suffering of the women who have been sold as sex slaves by Daesh.

While I was at the medical centre JP had taken under his wing an American lad who had flown in to join Dwekh. He had spent a couple of days taking him to the market, getting him kitted out, sorting his paperwork, etc. The next day JP was returning to the front, and told him: 'Hold fire in Duhok for the day, I'll get your clearance sorted with General Wahed, and you can join us tomorrow.'

When he got the clearance through he called the guy. 'Right, clearance all sorted, let's get you down here tomorrow.'

After a pause the guy replied: 'Yeah it's not for me, I am not going to come.'

'Where are you? We'll get something sorted out and deal with whatever is worrying you.'

'I'm actually back in Germany, waiting for my connecting flight to the States. Sorry.'

It turned out the guy had literally headed to the airport the minute JP had left him, without so much as a courtesy call. I had to wonder what went through the heads of people like him. Were they genuine but did the questioning at the airport, then the bargaining over weapons on the black market throw them off kilter, or was it the lack of five-star accommodation? Or was it just that they wanted to say they had been there, got the kit on, snapped a photo to impress everyone on Facebook, and that was their mission accomplished? They could head on back to their cosy homes, claiming to be a hero. There was a saying I came across from a volunteer I was to meet later that sadly seemed very apt to so many of these lads – 'Everyone wants to be a gangster, until it's time to do gangster shit.' In other words they love the image, but when the reality of the new life they've chosen kicks in, they're out of there before you know it.

The issue of these volunteer fighters reared its head in Syria around this time when *Pirates of the Caribbean* actor Michael Enright joined the fight out there with the YPG, only for Jordan Matson to speak out, claiming he was 'mentally unstable' and 'a liability'. He made a public plea for the US State Department to send someone out to collect Michael for his own, and everyone else's safety. I never met Michael first-hand so wouldn't like to judge, but I do know he denied those claims and there were clearly others who were happy fighting alongside him.

Then there were the crazy gung-ho volunteers, who most definitely had the guts, but who lacked any common sense. One guy was picked up just driving through the middle of Kurdistan on his own, waving his guns around, and announcing: 'I am off to find Daesh. I am here to kill those fuckers!'

It turned out he wasn't connected to any group, but had literally flown in, armed himself up, and was heading off on a one-man crusade against the enemy. The kid was only about eighteen, and after being stopped at a checkpoint was given to Dwekh to look after, but he lasted about a day before he headed off again.

Some volunteers just couldnt't fit in. I would hear the odd story about one guy who moved from group to group repeatedly getting thrown out. He liked to talk about fragging – throwing a grenade at someone on your own team that you want shot of. 'I'm going to frag so and so,' he would announce drunkenly, as everyone exchanged looks.

Another volunteer was at the front for a while but ended up living in a hotel. He still wanted to give the impression online that he was fighting the fight though, so he would post old pictures and pretend he was still at the front. People began to notice their own photographs and posts being copied by him and pasted as though they were his own. If anyone tried to flag it up he would block them and start a campaign of abuse against them. It was worrying to see, and I was concerned it would taint the image of the good people out there.

Before you think that everyone I came across out there was a nutter, I should add that there were plenty of great Western volunteers! Aside from those I got on with in Dwekh, I had contact with lots of great guys in other sections, and we would keep each other up to date and share news and tips. There was one group in particular I was in touch with who were initially called Brothers of Kurdistan but later changed their name to the Peshmerga International Detachment (IDET). There were some great fighters in their unit, which was based just outside the town of Kirkuk in north-east Iraq, and occasionally if someone contacted me about joining the fight who sounded like they would fit in better with IDET I would send them their way. One of their rules was that they only took ex-military personnel, so I knew I could never have joined them, but they were a good bunch.

Back in Baqofa we got stuck into more patrols with the General. We never did a crazy run of the entire front line with him again as we had the first night, but there were still plenty of tense moments and action-packed evenings. It was still Ramadan so the mortars were still coming in thick and fast, and we had to be on high alert at all times.

It wasn't always easy to stay alert though, as we could be sat for hours at a time and it was human nature to get tired and bored. One evening after several hours in the trench lying in the cold and dark, I told JP: 'Fuck this, I am getting my head down for a bit', and set myself up at the back of the trench. Just as I dozed off, my worst nightmare happened – I felt a scampering up my leg. Yelping, I was off that wall like a shot. 'A fucking mouse! Where is he?!' I yelled, backing up. JP was on the floor in tears. Turned out 'my kind friend' had waited until I was relaxed and slipping into sleep to run his fingers over my leg, imitating a mouse. Thanks, mate.

Sadly one night one of the Pesh guys was killed further down the line. Apparently he had put his head out of the trench to get a look at what was happening just as Dushka fire came in from the Daesh base in Batnaya, and it took him out.

His body was carried back to the front line and he was loaded into an ambulance which headed off to the nearby hospital. I hadn't known him but it was still a shock, and sad to see. While we were aware that there was always a very real risk of death on the front line, I suppose we had been there so often and all survived that it had begun to seem as though we were somehow immune. This put it firmly back into the front of our minds that we were not. Any of us could be killed any day.

Another evening soon after this, I did think our time had come, and we were going to get slotted ourselves. We were with the General down at the berm and had been sitting quietly for a while keeping an eye on things, when he decided we should move along a bit for a clearer view of an area that was concerning him. As we started to shift ourselves, the quiet was suddenly shattered as shots rang out around us. The sharp popping sound told me bullets were flying past just feet from my head, and adrenalin instantly pumping, we dived for cover, readying our rifles, to return fire. But the General started shouting – it wasn't Daesh starting an ambush, this was our own side shooting at us!

Some Peshmerga based further along the front line hadn't realized we were there, and on seeing movement had become a bit trigger happy and opened up before checking. I stared at the bullets lodged in the dirt around us that had missed us by a matter of feet. The shooters got a proper dressing down from the General, and we sighed with relief that their aim hadn't been good enough to get any direct hits on us. Turning to JP I remarked: 'Hopefully if Daesh do actually appear, our own side will perform a bit more accurately when it matters . . .'

Luckily the only time I actually had to go to the local medical centre was to accompany Big K. He loved his food and ate a lot, all the time, but didn't have a particularly strong stomach. One day he ate something that made him seriously ill so JP and I took him, groaning pathetically, to be treated. The medical centre was a community centre that had been converted because of its proximity to the front line, and was just two miles from Baqofa, five hundred metres past the first checkpoint as you were heading back to Duhok.

Big K was put on a drip to recover, and we enjoyed a

game of Tactical Table Tennis while we waited, on a ping-pong table still up in one of the rooms. Eventually he emerged, sheepish but much happier, and we headed home.

Around this time disturbing rumours began circulating that Daesh had access to chemical weapons. Initially reports came through that mustard gas had been used in Syria, and then over a cup of chai one day one of the Pesh soldiers told me, 'Daesh are using chemical weapons on us now, here in Kurdistan. They have attacked people north of Erbil, at the Mosul Dam. They think it is mustard gas.'

I was disturbed by the news, less out of a fear that it would be used on us than out of concern that innocent civilians would be targeted. The damage mustard gas can do to a person's skin and respiratory system is horrific. Yet again it proved to me the depths that these people would stoop to.

For the Kurds in particular, the idea of chemical weapons was terrifying, as they had suffered horrifically from them under Saddam's regime. Thousands were killed and thousands more left severely injured during the Iran–Iraq War in the 1980s. The idea that they could face this kind of attack again was a real low blow.

One of the lads visited a neighbouring village and came back with reports of strange injuries amongst the locals, in particular unexplained burns on their bodies. No one really knew if chemical weapons were the cause, or if paranoia and exaggeration were kicking in caused by escalating fear that the weapons were in existence.

I was sick and tired of the fact that the British government didn't seem to be stepping in to help in some way. I know it is always up for debate what level of involvement we take as a country in these situations, but there was no question that the UK's reticence was only helping to increase the confidence of Daesh. They seemed to think their intimidation was working and they were untouchable.

I'd have liked to have seen the British government sending troops in to do their bit and put a stop to Daesh once and for all, but at the very least, some funding and support for those of us who had headed out there, wouldn't have gone amiss. Despite trying to stick to my 'No RPG' rule I began to crack a little on the politics side, and began commenting on this aspect of things on my Facebook. I would reply to statements by the likes of David Cameron and Boris Johnson and eventually wrote an open letter to the Prime Minister. It said:

Please, for just once.....stop talking, stop wasting time, stop finding excuses.......HELP US HELP THESE PEOPLE !!!

In the time it has taken you to read this statement, you could have signed papers enabling millions of pounds worth of aid to be heading our way. You don't want to be the man that started another war, I get that ..... I really do, but we are out here, already, just a little help; is that too much to ask?

Whilst I am sure, somewhere in London, there's an over paid official whose job it is to read this and possible print it out for Mr. Cameron to read, I'm starting to think he may not actually get it. Each and every day, people from back home in the UK ask me what they can do to help.......so here's your chance.

Print this off, put it in an envelope, and go down to 10 Downing Street and give it to the guy on the gate, if you can't get there put it in the post, send it via carrier pigeon for all I care......we have asked for a reply time and time again, perhaps it's time we demanded one.

If, in the speeches you gave to gain the offices you now hold had you said, 'I intend to stand by and do nothing while the world goes to ruin, while innocent people are slaughtered, woman are raped and children are murdered, I intend to stand by and watch as some of my citizens stand up and say "enough is enough", and head out to do my job for me, without offering them aid or assistance. I intend to pretend that there is nothing to be done' would you have gained the position of power you now find yourself in?

I was told by hundreds of people that they had printed and sent the letter, and it was picked up by some online media outlets. A close friend who knows the inner workings of Parliament intimately, told me that there was no question that I would be known to the Prime Minister by this stage. Apparently news of the Westerners who had headed out to join the fight against Daesh have been the kind of thing to appear on his daily briefing sheet. I doubt I will ever know, but it would be nice to have received a response, and even nicer to think he might have taken on board some of my thoughts!

The nights a few weeks before when we had gone up to Alpha and Bravo roofs had led to discussions about how to do house clearance, and it flagged up a divide between British, American and Kurdish attitudes towards it.

I understood the American way of clearing, but only in the right place – back in the States, in a shopping mall full of people with suspected terrorists in it, it makes absolute sense. But in a war-torn village, with no civilians and just an old building to safeguard, it seemed daft. As I kept saying, whatever way the Kurds want to do it is how we should do it. I had come to Kurdistan not to lead, not to try and teach anyone anything, but to help. As I put it to Tex one day: 'If the General tells me to go and stand by that toilet over there and guard it for two weeks, I will do that without thinking I might know better. As I keep saying, I am not here to question things, but to stick to my basic motto: Do your job.'

The Brits on the whole shared my way of thinking, but not every Westerner who went out there thought the same.

There were definitely some who thought they knew best, and that they were there to teach the locals how to do things better and more efficiently – i.e. their way.

Marcus told me about an American who joined Dwekh after I briefly left for Turkey, who began trying to teach the locals how to clear a building his way. But they just weren't interested.

'Clearing a building room by room is a simple procedure, come on guys, let's be professional!' he would burst out at them, frustrated.

Marcus had shrugged and replied: 'If there is a building full of Daesh, we don't need to risk our lives clearing it. Why would we risk getting shot or stabbed? It is not our building, and it can be built again quickly.'

The guy wouldn't give up and kept discussing the importance of any evidence that could be salvaged.

The General got wind of the conversation, and seeing as this guy was so determined his way of doing things was right he sent him off with some of his men one afternoon to teach them the techniques. The guy took heart from this and spent a couple of hours getting them all to do it exactly his way. Then just as he had them trained to perfection, the General came down and called them out of the building.

Through the interpreter he said: 'This way of clearing a house would be wasting time and putting my men's lives at risk. This is how we do it.' With that he launched an RPG at the house, blowing it to pieces.

As he stalked off, chest puffed out even further than ever, there was nothing the guy could do but stare open-mouthed, while everyone else suppressed a grin . . .

10

DISILLUSIONED AND FRUSTRATED

As the months went on I was getting frustrated that we were still being told to hold the front line, and weren't able to push forward and actually attack Daesh, especially when they were sitting there, in our sights! But there were other issues coming to a head for me as well.

The tighter we were getting with the Pesh guys, and the more we were out and about, the more Ahmed seemed to want to reassert his role. There were several occasions when he would insist on us joining him in something that felt like a self-promotional excursion.

One properly hot day, after a long night on the front, we were having some downtime when one of the boys suggested going to a nearby dam for a swim. It was only fifteen minutes away and sounded perfect, exactly what we needed to cool down and unwind. So we told Ahmed our plan, and he said it was fine, but got the translator to tell us, 'We need to go to one of the more dangerous areas en route and do some things. You need to change out of your shorts and flip-flops, and into full gear.'

As instructions go, 'do some things' was a bit vague, and it was a nuisance getting kitted up, but assuming there was a reason for it, we did as we were told. Shortly afterwards, our truck, having stopped nowhere dangerous at all, pulled up outside Ahmed's house. Wandering around his garden, he pointed out an area and said: 'You can leave your kit here while we go for a swim.'

He kept looking round to his neighbours' houses while he was talking, and I was getting really hot, bothered and wound up.

'We are literally here and kitted up so he can parade us to his neighbours, like "look what I am in charge of!" He wants all our kit laid out here for everyone to look at and admire. Fuck this. Let's not bother going for a swim,' I said. With everyone else in agreement we stormed back to the truck, day ruined.

Another time he left a message saying we Westerners needed to go to Erbil to meet a member of Asayesh, the Kurdish military intelligence agency, and to be ready the next day at 10:00. He pulled up and we all traipsed round the back to climb in, but he waved us away.

'Get all your gear on before we go.'

'Why do we need that?' I asked, particularly suspicious after the swimming incident, and knowing that Erbil was most definitely not a place to go in full military uniform and with weapons. It may only be a couple of hours away from Baqofa, but the two places are worlds apart. Erbil is a fully functioning city, and you could expect a pretty similar reaction to walking around there all kitted up with guns as you'd get in Birmingham.

'We need to go via several places on the front line too,' Ahmed replied, listing off several villages.

Obligingly, we went back and grabbed vests, helmets, weapons, the works, and someone got the gimpy – the General-Purpose Machine Gun – on top of the truck and fully loaded. Needless to say, we didn't stop anywhere on the front line, but a couple of hours later, pulled up at a five-star hotel in Erbil. In retrospect we should have ripped all our kit off then and there. But instead we headed into the bar, where dignitaries were floating around, and people were enjoying quiet business meetings. The guy we were meeting looked taken aback at the sight of us, and the first thing he asked was: 'Why are you dressed like this?'

'We were told to.'

'Oh right! Well, I only wanted to meet you and say hello.'

It felt as if this was another example of Ahmed wanting to show off 'his boys' and tell the world 'look what I am in charge of'. For some reason he always seemed to need to prove himself. As far as I was concerned, he was doing a very bad job of it.

It got worse too – not only did we feel like dicks, but it was clear we were making people uneasy, and eventually other Asayesh approached us and asked to leave not just the hotel, but the city! We were lucky not to be arrested as carrying weapons in Erbil, especially so openly, really is a no-go. We were embarrassed and furious with Ahmed, muttering mutinously amongst ourselves, as we clambered back into the truck.

On the way back we had to pass through a number of checkpoints and, concerned about the bad feeling we had left behind us in the city, Ahmed didn't want to stop at any of them.

'We are to travel down the outside lane with the sirens and beepers going,' he decided. 'I am going to drive through all the checkpoints as though we have to be somewhere important, and don't stop.'

'No, no, no, no, no!' we all shouted at him, already at our wits' end and ready to dump him out of the truck. 'That is clearly a way to get shot. Approach in a civilized manner, explain the confusion, and get them to radio ahead to the next checkpoint to explain.'

Full speed at a checkpoint indeed. What was wrong with the man?

Then another issue reared its head in the form of two new volunteers. Manny had taken JP, Marcus and me out for lunch with a couple of guys who wanted to join us, two Americans called Oliver and Thomas. Oliver came from a deeply religious background, and kept quoting passages from the Bible. He told me, 'My daughter was recently killed in a car crash. I want to fight Daesh and do something really important and decent with my life.'

Thomas explained that he was a member of a group called Veterans Against ISIS, which was looking at getting ex-military personnel out to the fight. He said: 'We have massive sponsorship, and I have put my entire life into this. We are really well known back in the States, so it would be great to be on board.'

We asked them to stay in a hotel for a couple of days while we made some checks. On the drive back, JP said to me: 'Get this. Thomas asked me: "What's the chick situation in Baqofa, mate?" I said, "It's the front line, mate, there aren't any." He then winked and told me he would be more an admin kind of guy back in town, then. What a fucking dick. What does he think he is coming out here for?'

I looked into them a bit further and it was true that VAI were gaining a reputation in the US, so would potentially come with good funding. But then I got a message from a friend at IDET: 'If you take Thomas and Oliver we can't have any communication with you any more. Whether that is passing on possible soldiers, exchanging news about developments in the fight around the country, or even idle chat. It might sound extreme, but we have our reasons.'

This left us in a difficult position, and we decided we would need to go back into town to discuss the issues with them, but I was getting a bad feeling about this one.

To throw another negative into the pile, it was becoming increasingly obvious that the locals, who in the beginning had been grateful and desperate for help in any form, were starting to see the money that was coming along with the volunteers, and were beginning to take advantage. One of the local boys asked me to tell some arriving volunteer Frenchmen that they needed to hand the taxi driver 160,000 dinar when he collected them in Erbil for the journey to Duhok.

'What for?' I asked, knowing full well the cost was 80,000 dinar, having done the journey myself numerous times. It was an annoying trip, with the route much more complicated than it would have been during peacetime. The fastest route would have seen you going along main roads travelling west then north, passing through Mosul on the way. But of course this was now a no-go area, so the route was along much smaller roads, going north first, and then west, to be sure of steering clear of Daesh-controlled areas. Inevitably these tiny country roads made the journey slower, but Dwekh used the same driver each time, a guy known as Crazy Taxi, who was an Assyrian Christian and very supportive of their work, so he gave a good price.

'This is how we do it now,' the guy replied. 'We have set up a new procedure for every arriving volunteer, and that is part of it.'

I was angry, as it was basically the group making money off these volunteers. It felt much worse than tourists arriving at the airport of holiday destinations and being charged double just for their naivety.

'They are here to help you!' I exploded. 'At the very

most they should be charged cost price, you shouldn't be making money off them!'

But that was met with shrugs, and it was as though he genuinely couldn't see what was wrong. I started to wonder if I had been partly at fault. I had been so easy-going with my money, giving it out all over the place and paying for things without a question, that I could see that he might think it meant nothing to me. The reality was that I was worried that I wasn't doing enough to help everyone there, and that money was an important way I knew I could make a difference. Financially I was better off than most people I had met out here, but I didn't have bottomless pockets, and nor did the other Westerners – but it was clear this was something the Dwekh boys had begun to think . . . I resolved then and there to be more careful who I helped out with money and who I didn't.

Lying in bed that night I thought back over my five months in Kurdistan and realized I was feeling disillusioned and frustrated.

I was particularly bored of coming across people with other agendas. I just wanted to fight to help people live a free and peaceful life, without the dark cloud of Daesh hanging over them, but it felt like there were issues getting in the way at every turn. I began seriously questioning if I was achieving enough out here to make everything I had sacrificed for it worthwhile. I had given up a great life in the UK and accepted that I might even die in this fight. But I had thought Daesh would be the only real problem I would be facing, not those who were supposedly on the same side as me. I finally drifted off to sleep, unsure of my future plans, and wondering if my time here was done.

The next night we were due to do a tour of the churches in surrounding villages. It was a Sunday evening, and the increased threat of attack during Ramadan meant that the Christians were particularly afraid to go to their services, but still wanted to keep up their normal lives as much as possible. We decided to go round in a hearts and minds style role to reassure them. Nothing heavy-handed or in their faces, but just a patrol and a few words of reassurance.

It was going to be an intense twenty-four hours – after the churches we were due on the front line, then we were going to head back and see Oliver and Thomas.

Ahmed insisted on coming with us, and it proved to be quite a successful evening. We did feel as if we had put at least some of the locals' minds at ease. Then we went on to the front line for a night of mortars until the sun came up, then got ready to head back to Duhok to see our two visitors. There was just one problem. Ahmed, who was insistent we couldn't travel on without him, decided he wanted to sleep and expected us to do the same, despite the fact Thomas and Oliver were waiting for us at the other end. At this stage he wanted to join us in everything we did, and so without his permission we were not allowed to push ahead with the task at hand.

I was tired, frustrated and at my limit. I was putting all my money, heart and soul into this mission, and yet the likes of Ahmed seemed as if they wanted to help only when it suited them and entirely on their own terms. I couldn't understand their reasoning.

Remembering the thoughts going round and round in my head the night before, I knew that right now I wasn't happy and I didn't think this was worth it.

'I'm leaving,' I announced.

'Wind your neck in, Big T,' JP laughed.

'I'm serious, mate, I am at my limit. Too many people are taking the piss and we are not being allowed to achieve what we need to.'

JP looked at me shocked, but realizing I was serious, he nodded, a bit of him knowing what I was going through.

'I need out of here and to work out what I really want to do. Maybe I'll be back, but for now, this is it.'

Once I'd made my decision, I knew it was the right choice. Packing my bags, I said my goodbyes, instructing everyone to look after Rocky until I could sort something out for him, and caught a cab to Erbil. I was on my way out of there, but couldn't believe I had done it. Was I going to regret it? Quite possibly, but at that moment I knew I was going to explode if I didn't leave. I didn't even know what my long-term plans were to be, but I decided to fly back to the UK and regroup.

Landing back at Heathrow I was nervous about the reception I would get. I was fairly confident that fighting alongside Dwekh rather than YPG should have kept me the right side of the law, but the rules weren't completely clear-cut. Sure enough, as I made my way through the security checks, I was pulled to one side and asked to follow a member of staff into a side room for questioning. For two hours a member of Special Branch asked me all sorts of questions about where I had been, what I had done, who I had spoken with, what my motives were, etc. It was clear he wanted to know that I hadn't been radicalized in any way. My phone was also taken away for checking. He was perfectly nice about it, and I was more than happy to answer all his questions. It was actually reassuring that they were keeping tabs on anyone who had gone out there to fight, and were making sure they were at least on the right side! He didn't directly say it, but the impression he gave me was that he was thinking, 'Good on you, glad to see someone is going out there to fight.'

For the first few days it was nice to be back. Catching up with people, eating my favourite food, going to the gym and sleeping in a room all to myself were all luxuries I had sorely missed.

I was shocked by the press interest in me, though – I had calls and messages from all sorts of newspapers, TV shows and radio shows, not just in the UK, but around the world. They were asking to interview me on life out in Iraq, as well as my motivations for going and coming back. I turned them all down, as I didn't think my story was yet over. I also worried about putting myself out there so publicly in terms of the safety of those close to me, when I would have no real control over what was being written. And I didn't want to make myself a bigger target when I did return to Iraq, which I felt sure was on the cards.

Interestingly though, one of the papers, the *Sun*, was not going to give up when I turned down the chance for a front-page interview. A week later I saw Jimbo on the front of the paper telling his story instead! I am not sure how happy he was about the headline, though: 'Granddad v Jihadi'. He is officially a granddad, but he is in his fifties, so tries to avoid that tagline. Unluckily for him it was used in the headline of every paper that then picked up on his story. It was a good piece in terms of raising awareness for people heading out to fight the cause, but I felt no regret that I hadn't taken up the chance to have it written about me.

My delight at being back home wore off within days, and it was as though I had reverse culture shock. I kept getting annoyed with Brits for what felt like an inability to see beyond petty problems in their own lives. I remember standing in McDonald's one day and a woman complaining to the guy behind the counter that her chips were a bit cold. I could feel annoyance building in me as she went on and on, and had to stop myself exploding: 'You think it's worth kicking off about cold chips when there are people in Iraq being slaughtered on a daily basis? I bet if I asked you about them, you would just shrug. Get your priorities right, you idiot!'

I know it wasn't her fault, but I was feeling removed from life here. It felt as if no one genuinely understood what was happening in Iraq, and everyone was just getting on with their lives, heads buried in the sand. It was only when I was chatting to JP or Tex on WhatsApp, and hearing the stories of everything happening back in Kurdistan, that things felt real.

Often I would try and talk to my friends about world events, and they would have no opinion, or say they hadn't thought about it and would shrug it off as something happening in a far off place, which I was incredulous about.

The one thing that did get people talking, though, was the shootings on the beach in Tunisia, which happened a few days after I arrived home. It pushed the issue to the forefront of a lot of people's minds, and suddenly they did want to discuss it. I sadly wasn't surprised by the events, as I had thought tourists would eventually be targeted, although my prediction had been Turkey rather than North Africa. It was a shame that Brits had to be directly caught up in the horrors of Daesh before some people were able to give it their full attention, not that even that put us all on the same wavelength. I was forever having disagreements with people about whether the UK should be getting involved militarily or not. I believed that it was ridiculous that our army was holding back, and it was angering me that the government were so clearly afraid to get involved.

I likened it to our reaction to Hitler and the Nazi movement. In the same way that back then we were scarred from World War One and avoided intervening when Hitler's actions became increasingly aggressive and even genocidal, now we were damaged by the effects of our previous involvement in Afghanistan and the Middle East. What had effectively been an unsatisfactory outcome there, combined with all the army lives lost, meant British people were on the whole fiercely against involvement. But as with Nazi Germany, I saw Daesh as different, and dangerous to ignore. This wasn't a group who were fighting another internal battle, this was a group with huge similarities to Nazism. Daesh were fanatics, who were busy ethnically cleansing, doing their best to provoke other countries and see how far they could push it before anyone would interfere, and ultimately not only wanted to rule in their country, but had their eye on the rest of the world. To me it was imperative they were stopped now, before things went even further.

I wasn't at odds with everyone, though – a lot of people came and congratulated me and commended anyone who was willing to go out and fight. They weren't always people I knew, some of them had read my initial stories in the paper, or followed me online. I even had people come up and give me money in the street to go towards Improve the Situation, and one guy in my local gym very generously gave me £1,000 for the cause.

But ultimately I realized the UK no longer felt like home, and I couldn't find my place in it. Right now I knew I needed to be back in that fight against Daesh. It didn't sound as though things had improved at Dwekh, though, and JP told me it was proving harder and harder to do anything useful. While I was in the UK Tex decided he had had enough of it, and flew back to the US. Like me he had become concerned at the number of barriers that seemed to be put in the way of pushing ahead in the fight and getting rid of Daesh once and for all. Tex and I have kept in close contact since, and he is going to be a friend for life. He follows all the goings-on very closely, and as I write this, is considering heading off to help the fight elsewhere, or staying in the States and moving into law enforcement.

Jimbo too had left the group, and headed home to Newcastle. It was clear from social media, though, that his heart was still with Dwek and I won't be surprised if I see him head back out to the fight sometime soon.

The other reason I was furious with Dwekh was over Rocky. When I came back I had asked the boys to look out for him while I researched getting him transferred to the UK. He was my little buddy, and I felt like I had abandoned him when I had left, and wanted to get him over here with me. I started to get the ball rolling, but when the time came for JP to get him moved to Erbil, Rocky had gone missing. It emerged that there had been a row between some of the locals and the Westerners about the money and time I was willing to put into getting Rocky moved to the UK, and the locals had been angry and resentful about it. I was furious and sad at the idea that his disappearance could have had anything to do with one of them. I had to hope he was off doing his own thing but I couldn't help the doubts in my head. If I ever found anything untoward had happened to my little pal . . .

So I began researching other groups out in Iraq and

Syria, and put out some feelers. I tried to get hold of Jordan, but he had married a Lebanese girl, and was involved in moving their life to the US by then.

The positive thing was that I was getting a lot of offers coming in from people who had seen that I wasn't just all talk, and had actually gone out there and done something, not just written about wanting to on my Facebook wall. I was even offered a role fighting alongside a team in Nigeria who were tackling Boko Haram. There was a real appeal to that, as I think they are in the same scum league as Daesh, and in fact earlier in 2015 they had pledged their allegiance to their fellow terrorist group. Boko Haram members have killed over 20,000 people since their emergence, displaced 2.3 million people from their homes, and need quelling as much as Daesh. As with Daesh they appeared to have a particular hatred of Westerners, and their name actually translates roughly as 'Western education is forbidden'. You were no longer safe visiting countries where they were based. This was not just two distant countries suffering a problem, it was affecting us. But ultimately I decided I had already put myself through a much steeper learning curve than most volunteer fighters, and it wasn't the time to start on another. I had accumulated an understanding of Kurdish people, culture, and their way of fighting, not to mention started to carve a reputation in their country, so it would make more sense to build on that by returning to Kurdistan.

Then I caught up with Steve Costa, the guy who had set up IDET. The group were based over in Kirkuk, a town about eighty kilometres south of Erbil. We had now been in touch for a few months, and I continued to admire the work they were doing from afar. The appeal for me was in the close working relationship they had with the Pesh in their area – they were on the same base, and went out on missions with them regularly, and essentially they seemed to be taken more seriously than Dwekh was by our Peshmerga over in Baqofa. They had cleared a dozen villages of Daesh in recent months, and seemed to be pushing forward, rather than just holding a line, exactly what I was keen to be doing. I also liked the fact that another guy I had been chatting to who was with them, a northern lad called Baz, was often hard to get hold of as he was so busy. It wouldn't always be that he was off fighting, sometimes he was just out buying washing machines – but even that was a sign that they thought they were really in it for the long haul. They weren't just spending their downtime sat on the sofa, and the organized side of it sounded right up my street.

I had never considered that I could join them though, as they had a strict rule of only taking ex-military. But while chatting on WhatsApp one day back in the UK, Steve said, 'There is a bed space here for you if you want it. We will happily take you. You may not have served in the military, but being out here has given you more valuable experience of the fight than a lot of ex-soldiers will have. You know the people, the culture, the politics, and basic fighting skills. We would seriously be happy to have you.'

I had a good think about it. It was a great compliment to hear that, and I knew my following was probably also appealing to them, in terms of donations and getting them put on the map a bit. I decided this would be the next place for me.

To prove I was serious – and let's face it, to ingratiate myself in advance, in the hope of a decent bed! – I spent a good few hundred quid on food parcels filled with anything I thought they might be missing, and sent them out. Requests included everything from Twining's Earl Grey tea bags to protein bars.

I also decided there was one extra-crucial piece of kit I needed to take back with me this time – a respirator in case of a chemical attack. I researched online and bought an S-10, which was previously used by the British Army, and then I got hold of a GSR – General Service Respirator, which the army have now replaced the S-10s with. I figured it was not something to skimp on when it could save my life, and following what the army over here considered to be the best piece of equipment was the smartest move.

It was now the start of September, and the papers were filled with the story of Aylan Kurdi, the little Kurdish refugee boy washed up on the beach in Turkey. This caused a huge backlash from the public about the lack of support being given to refugees, which I was glad to see, but even then, I felt the responses were often short-sighted. It was a very knee-jerk reaction, demanding that we take in more refugees. This was not something I disagreed with – I think we should help every person in trouble that we possibly can. When there is a humanitarian crisis on this scale it is the responsibility of humankind to react to do whatever they can to help out.

But it was as though people weren't looking to the real root of the problem, why these people were fleeing their homes in the first place. Dealing with the reason these people felt forced to make these horrifically dangerous trips would do a lot more than just putting a sticking plaster on the problem. People will generally choose to stay in their own countries if they feel safe and secure, but while Daesh still exists, that will not happen. Obviously Daesh are only part of the picture, particularly in Syria, but they are the worst part of the picture. Get rid of them and it will make a huge difference.

I hoped that people would see this aspect of the argument, and I put a picture of Aylan as the wallpaper on my phone as a reminder as to one of the reasons I needed to push ahead with this fight.

I had just one more job to do while I was back in the UK – get a couple of tattoos done that represented things of importance to me. I booked into Soul Rise studio in central London, and had my blood type tattooed on my chest over my heart. Then I had 'Age Officium Tuum' written over my shoulders: the Latin for my motto, 'Do Your Job', something I intended to continue doing.

11

RETURN TO THE FRONT LINE

I got to Heathrow Airport several hours before my flight, which was via Turkey, and checked in. But no sooner had I boarded the plane and sat down in my seat than two border control guards came on board and approached me. After checking my passport and ticket they asked me to accompany them off the plane. I could see all the other passengers watching me nervously, wondering what I had done. I was then met by someone from Special Branch and questioned for two hours again. The questions were similar to the last time – how much money I was taking out, what I was planning on doing, more of what I had seen previously, and my motives for returning to the country. Again, all totally understandable questions, and I was glad their checks were so thorough for people taking this particular route. Hopefully this would stop anyone off to fight for the wrong side.

The only downside was that I missed my flight, and

had to wait a full day until the next plane, by which point I was beginning to feel a bit like Victor Navorski, in the film *The Terminal*, wandering round, trying to find entertainment and a way to refresh!

I flew back to Erbil filled with excitement and trepidation. I couldn't wait to get stuck in again and do my bit, and I had high hopes for IDET, whose work and reputation had really appealed to me. But I was nervous too, as I knew I would be the least qualified of everyone there, and while Steve had said my experience meant I was on a par with them, I still felt I needed to prove myself to the others.

I also realized just how easily I had adapted to a soldier's lifestyle out there, and not for the first time, I wished I had tried harder to pursue the army as a career. It was a shame it had taken me until thirty-eight years old to be able to do what I had always dreamed of. But at least I was doing it.

In passport control, the guard saw my papers that explained my reason for being there, and put his hand through the window to shake my hand and welcome me back to the country. Such a noticeable difference from the first time, and I couldn't help grinning. As usual, customs was never simple though. As my 120 kilos of bags went through the X-ray machines one was pulled aside. The officials wanted to look at my scope – or 'zoom' as they referred to it.

'For day or night?' the guard questioned me.

'Normal day scope,' I assured him, but he still insisted

on calling his supervisor over. The first time this had happened I was worried, now I was just impatient to get the whole rigmarole over with.

The supervisor shook my hand after looking at my papers.

'Welcome back, Mr Tim.' Then, turning to his subordinate, he said something in Kurdish in a harsh tone, cuffed him round the head and walked off! Needless to say I got my scope and headed on my way, amused at this almost comical re-entry and the unfortunate guards who seemed to work in each airport.

The plan was to stay in Erbil for a week and arrange some paperwork and get extra gear for the guys. I got to the hotel and after dropping my stuff went to meet Baz in a place called T Bar, which is an American sports bar in the city that's full of ex-pats and is popular with some locals too. Along with a pub called the German Bar, it was the place I was most likely to do any socializing when back in the city. Baz was forty-one, from the north of England, and told me he had served with the Royal Artillery. He had spent a few months fighting with YPG in Syria before heading to Kirkuk, but told me: 'Despite all the news reports making you think otherwise, there was very little action to get involved in over in Syria. I thought I would come over here and try my hand with these guys instead. So far so good.'

I always felt very at home and relaxed in Erbil. I think Brits lazily and incorrectly bunch the whole of the Middle East together, and assume everyone in the region will have similar attitudes and lifestyles. The reality is that Kurds are not so different to the West in their way of life. The majority of people in Erbil were well-educated, kind and liberal, and friendly towards foreign visitors. The women occasionally wear headscarves, but even those are few and far between, and they socialize and chat freely with men, even mixing in the bars and drinking alcohol.

Even the fact there are bars at all sets Kurdistan apart from the rest of Iraq, where the stricter Arab culture generally dictates that the few places selling alcohol – even in a city like Baghdad – are to be found only inside hotels.

Lots of people fleeing Daesh in the surrounding towns and villages had headed to Erbil, but many of them found it too expensive to stay. Like any city around the world, life there is more expensive than the countryside, and for people who have already left so much behind, setting up in Erbil is beyond their means. Others had managed to make their way in the city, though, and had drawn a line under their past to such an extent that you often wouldn't even know what they had gone through at the hands of Daesh.

An example of this had occurred on one of my trips to the city, when I had been checking into my hotel, and the receptionist had begun making polite chat, 'What brings you to our country?'

I told her about my time in Kurdistan so far, and she smiled. 'Ah yes, now I recognize you from a news report I saw on the Westerners with Dwekh Nawsha. I just did not recognize you in different clothes, as I suppose I did not expect to meet you.'

We discussed where I was based, and the fighting happening at the front line, and she nodded. 'I am originally from Al-qosh, I know the area well, and its troubles.'

I pursued the conversation and she told me: 'My family and I had to flee the area because of the fighting. We left our old lives behind because Daesh gave us no choice, we wanted to survive. Some of my family have gone to stay with other family and friends in different villages and towns, but I wanted to come here. I have set up a new life here for myself.'

It was striking how resolute she was in the face of everything she had gone through, but also that I would never have known her story if I hadn't mentioned the area where she grew up. But that is how it was in Erbil – practically everyone in the city had been affected by Daesh in some way, either directly or indirectly, but they didn't want to dwell on their personal experiences. Instead it was a case of onwards and upwards with life, as though discussing the damage Daesh had caused would give power to the enemy. The city had a very positive vibe, despite the fact that the enemy had been just forty kilometres away at one stage in early 2015, before Peshmerga fighters had forced them back.

At the same time there was a sense of national pride about the way the Kurds were handling the fight with Daesh. Their bravery in the face of this terror, and their strength in tackling the enemy where others had been failing, had gained them respect on a world stage. The Kurds were noticing this and while people didn't like to dwell on their individual experiences, there was a sense of 'Look what we are still doing' on a larger scale, that was representative of the patriotism of their nation. They were keen to capitalize on the recognition at a time when their fight to be a recognized country was still ongoing.

Over the next few days we canvassed various people for help, and they were all so generous. Staff in the Life Support Team hospital – who had treated me when I had food poisoning – were hugely generous with medical equipment to help out, so much in fact that we struggled to carry it all back to the hotel. Then we met this great Kurdish body-builder called Ahmed Majeed – or Ahmed Rambo as he calls himself. He has been key in instigating the gym culture in Kurdistan as a pastime for the young men, and gave us some gym stuff to train with in our downtime at the IDET compound. It was really sound of him, and he made it very clear how supportive he was of the cause.

I did a day trip to my old stomping ground to see the Dwekh boys and collect some of my weapons that were still there. I collected a pram I had previously posted out that was waiting in the DHL office, and took it to one of the locals who had just had a baby with his wife. He was really happy with the gift, and it was nice to see that people were still able to continue with a normal family life, despite everything going on around them. It was brilliant to meet up with all the old crew – although they were less impressed when they realized I wasn't staying.

Back in Erbil, I came across a little Anatolian puppy wandering the streets, looking hungry, dirty, and in need of some attention. I instantly thought of Rocky, and wondered if this little chap could fill the gap a bit. I called him Ollie, but after hanging out with him for a few hours, I realized I couldn't take him to the hotel. A British mate who runs an NGO out there agreed to look after him for a few days.

I squeezed in a bit of downtime too, grabbing a couple of the World Cup Rugby games, and meeting a friend in TGI Fridays – one of the best places to eat in the city. Ex-pats tend to stick together a lot, and being a small community they try and introduce you to others, so although I was rarely in Erbil, I still had a network of people I knew. This meal was with a friend who worked in oil and gas, but he was late for the meal, having suffered a typical Kurdish taxi experience. What inevitably happens is you climb in, ask to go somewhere and double check: 'You know where that is, right?' 'Yes, mister,' comes the firm reply. A minute later the driver is on the phone chatting to a friend, then hands over the phone, and a voice in broken English would ask: 'Where you need to go, mister?'

No driver would ever admit to not knowing a place, and they generally didn't speak English well enough, even if you could navigate them to your end point. On this particular evening my friend had become frustrated at going round in circles and not arriving at TGIs, as despite knowing where it was himself, the driver couldn't understand his directions. Eventually I looked up from my phone to see my friend driving himself into the car park, with the taxi driver in the passenger seat! Completely ridiculous, but not surprising to anyone who has spent time out there. The driver even followed us into TGIs, unashamedly insisting on being paid . . .

I was trying to spend time with other ex-pats I knew in Erbil, rather than Baz, whose girlfriend had flown out to Erbil to see him. One night she called me crying hysterically to say they had rowed and he had thrown her out of the hotel with no money. They eventually sorted things out, but when I asked him the next morning, 'Everything all right?' he seemed surprised and chatted on as though nothing had happened. We were due to go and join the group, so I decided I couldn't dwell on it for now, but it raised a bit of a flag to me about his potential future behaviour.

IDET's base was on a compound ten kilometres south of the city of Kirkuk, where they lived and fought alongside the 70th Peshmerga Unit. I called a taxi driver who had been pretty helpful over the last week and asked him if he could get hold of a vehicle to take us and all our equipment on the two-hour drive. He produced a truck with a flatbed on the back, and in everything went – gym stuff, medical supplies, body armour, dog food, and of course Ollie! – then we were on our way.

On the journey, Baz explained to me the hierarchy as far as we were concerned. At the top was Sheikh Jafar Mustafa, a former Peshmerga minister. Still a major player in the Kurdistan Regional Government, he was heavily involved in the military action, and headed up the 70th Unit, who dealt with everything happening around Kirkuk.

Next beneath him was the Lieutenant, a Kurdish guy called Akam, who had learnt English by translating for US troops during previous conflicts. Baz told me he had a strong American accent, and referred to everyone as 'motherfuckers'!

Then in IDET itself an American called Rupert was in charge, having taken over from the original founder, Steve, who had recently left. Rupert had been a captain in the US Army, and on Steve's departure there had been a vote amongst the group as to who should take over, and Rupert had seemed the natural choice, given his previous experience. He had asked Baz to suss me out while we were in Erbil, to make sure I was totally legit, and not out there to make money and create an image for myself, or with some other agenda altogether.

We pulled up at a compound which consisted of a huge house and courtyard, surrounded by prefab buildings that had been created especially for the Peshmerga, and now IDET too. The house used to belong to Ali Hassan al-Majid, or Chemical Ali as he was better known. He had served under Saddam Hussein – and was also his cousin – and had treated Kurdish people horrifically. He used all sorts of punishments on them, everything from deportation to mass killings and, most famously, chemical weapons, hence his nickname. After his arrest, the house was confiscated and there was something poetic about it being a useful base for the Kurds in their current battle. A part of me wished Chemical Ali was around to see it.

Heading in I was introduced to the guys, thirteen other Westerners, all of them American except Baz, and aged between twenty-five and forty-five. They were all ex-military as I had expected, apart from one guy called Tyler. He had fought alongside Baz for YPG in Syria, so like me was considered to have had enough experience. Baz had been able to vouch for him as a good and experienced team player when he had decided to move over to Kurdistan.

One guy with a goatee and glasses called Kidd introduced himself as second in command, and pulled me to one side for a bit of a pep talk.

'You need to be here for the right reasons,' he said. 'We keep a close eye on what everyone is up to, and there are no photos. We have a prison cell for people who aren't behaving, and we will use it. We recently stuck a couple of idiots in it.'

'That's fine, mate,' I said. 'I'm here to do my bit, not to do anything wrong. My main motivation is to stop Daesh and that's it.'

I was a bit irritated that he seemed to be doubting that, but knew that I was soon going to prove him wrong if he did think badly of me. I hardly needed the threat of a prison cell! But I relaxed a bit when one of the lads told me a story that explained why they were uptight and on edge at that moment. Just a few weeks before, a guy had turned up with all the right credentials. He seemed to be no problem, just put his head down and got on with it.

Then on the last day someone spotted him taking photos of himself in press body armour and a press helmet. He was pulled to one side, and asked: 'What the fuck are you doing?'

'It's just my cover story to get here in the first place,' he had tried to claim.

But the lads went through his stuff, and he had press cards, notes, and thousands of photos of all sorts of private areas, plans, people and equipment that would have seriously compromised IDET if they had been published or got into the wrong hands. There were volunteers there who if their pictures were released would be jailed back in their own countries, photographs of the buildings that would help enemies target an attack, and so on. So they stuck the guy in the jail cell while they worked out what to do. Eventually they destroyed all his memory sticks and cards, drove him down to the garage where he could get a taxi to Erbil, and basically told him to wind his neck in and never to try anything so sly again. I was told he was lucky as some of the local guys were convinced he was a spy rather than press, and wanted to shoot him. I understood their fury even if he was press – a lot of people are there to fight Daesh for their own reasons, but it doesn't mean they want the world to know about it. A journalist like this one is failing to respect that and can compromise lives.

I was to share a bedroom with Baz and three Americans, then given a tour of the rest of the building, which mainly consisted of a store room, more bedrooms and a small gym area, where our new equipment was welcomed with open arms.

I was thanked by the guys for the parcels I had sent over in advance, and we just relaxed for the rest of the afternoon. I exchanged stories and chatted a bit but I could see they had the same sense I had got at times in Dwekh, of people coming and going so often that you don't go out of your way with the new guys in the beginning, in case they don't last long!

Ollie settled in quickly too, running round exploring with Baz's dog, a great big mutt called Max, and a couple of others called Rose and Charlie.

That first evening I was told that we would be heading out on a mission the next night, preparing to take back some villages from Daesh. Then there would be an airstrike on the villages overnight to take out as many members of Daesh as possible and to destroy the buildings, and we would go in the morning after to finish everything off.

We spent all the next day getting ready – weapons cleaned and loaded, bags packed, all vehicles checked to ensure they were in working order. The other boys were quite relaxed and were joking around, while still taking their tasks seriously, but I was counting down the minutes, and couldn't wait to get on our way and get stuck in. I was happy I had only been with the group a matter of hours and we were already being sent out on a job.

'Why are we going out the night before, though?' I asked, knowing that we were only a few kilometres from the front line.

'We need to get to the front and get a good spot for the following morning,' Baz replied. 'When the road opens up and we go, it is gonna be a proper bun fight, trust me.'

Kidd added: 'We have cleared a dozen villages over the last few weeks. It has been good pushing forward and actually seeing results. Believe me, you are going to enjoy this!'

We were each assigned a vehicle, and I was put in an MRAP – a big mine-resistant, ambush-protected, troop-carrying vehicle – with Rupert driving and another guy up front, and three in the back, including me. I was impressed by Rupert, who seemed to be very switched on and a natural leader. The others were divided between three large Humvees and a smaller one, then off we set.

After driving for about twenty-five minutes, we pulled up at a berm in the middle of nowhere, and sure enough over the next few hours, more and more vehicles started appearing. When word got out there was going to be an offensive, anyone and everyone wanted to get involved. Old Pesh guys sitting at home around their fireplace would grab their rifles off the wall and head down, and young guys bundled into cars with mates to come along to join in the fight. Basically everyone felt so angry at Daesh that anyone who hadn't fled the area but had stayed to fight was not going to miss an opportunity to stick it to them.

We tried to get some sleep – two of the guys on the roof, two on the bonnet and me on the back seat, which given they were all bucket seats with a place for your rifle wasn't too comfy. Just as I was dozing off I heard jets flying low overhead, and climbing out of the vehicle saw flashes of light just a few kilometres away, followed by the muffled bang of explosions. The airstrikes were happening, preparing for our clean-up the next morning. I watched, thrilled that I was involved in this kind of operation, and hoping the targets were being taken out. When the attack ended I managed to get my head down for a couple of hours, before waking to see even more vehicles had arrived. Tanks, trucks, ambulances and cars, all jostling to get as close as possible to the gap in the berm that led to the road. I watched it all while eating breakfast. It was surreal, and if it wasn't for the weapons, I might have thought we were all here setting up for an early Sunday morning car-boot sale!

Several mine-clearance teams went ahead so we could get the mission underway. The frequency of the explosions showed just how many IEDs Daesh had planted on this stretch of road. I thought of all the pictures I had seen of people killed or maimed walking or driving over IEDs, and shuddered, impressed by the guys who bravely took on the job of finding and detonating them.

I began kitting up, knowing it couldn't be long now until we got the all-clear. Then a Volvo Estate pulled up a hundred metres over from us. Instantly people began heading for it. The driver jumped out and opened his boot, which was bulging with fridges. Pulling out an old wallet full of money, he began selling KitKats and cans of Red Bull. I started laughing in amazement, and turning to the lads, commented, 'This is crazy. It's like being on a building site when the snack wagon turns up!' I've got to give the guy his due, even in the middle of war he had spotted a gap in the market and jumped on it.

The boys started passing the time by telling me about previous village clearances, and one explained: 'We went on one crazy mission where some Daesh were attacking, but they got tangled up in some barbed wire. That area is now called the "body berm".'

Suddenly, though, word came back that the first half of the road had been cleared, and we were on the move. Baz hadn't been joking about it being like a bun fight – everyone was trying to get through the same tiny gap onto the road, and there was shouting, and horns blaring, and cars jostling . . . proper mental behaviour. But we pushed on through, getting into single file once we were on the road, as freestyling off-road would not only be harder driving, but would be very dangerous in terms of where IEDs may have been laid. We stopped again at the halfway point about two kilometres along the road. It was mid-morning by now, and I looked back at the huge queue of vehicles stretching into the distance behind us. The hatred for the enemy ahead was palpable.

A vehicle began driving alongside the road, stopping every twenty cars or so. As it got closer I saw that it was a chow wagon, and a Pesh guy was jumping out to serve up a free lunch. They certainly knew how to look after the people fighting for them, and as I sat under the MRAP eating it with a couple of the boys, I decided they had served up the best chicken and rice I had eaten in the country.

Occasionally an explosion would go off ahead where the teams were still clearing. We kept moving on slowly, and eventually cut across no-man's-land to a different road and pulled into a compound. We were sitting there waiting on instructions when suddenly word came through that some Pesh troops were pinned down by Daesh on the far side of the village and needed help.

'Come on, motherfuckers,' the Lieutenant shouted to IDET, 'let's go rescue these men.'

As he set off running to the vehicles, none of us needed any encouragement to follow him. We had spent twenty-four hours building up to this. Adrenalin pumping, I sprinted after him, oblivious to the weight of my weapons.

The Lieutenant's truck led the way along the road and over sandy hills, followed by the armoured Humvee, our MRAP, then the two other Humvees behind. The route was rough, and sent me and all the equipment bouncing into each other in the back, but we needed to get round the village to the long road on the far side as fast as possible.

Suddenly there was a huge bang and a cloud of dust shot up in the air, completely enveloping the vehicle in front. We slammed to a stop, everyone shouting, 'IED! IED!' Rupert quickly radioed through to them, getting crackled shouts back in response through the receiver. At least they were alive.

We all jumped out and ran over to find the front of the vehicle had been blown clean off, and the rest of it was totally destroyed, but incredibly all the boys climbed out unharmed.

Inspecting the road we could see it was an IED that had caused the damage. The Lieutenant had been lucky to avoid it just a few seconds before, and our vehicle, just five metres behind this one, would have stood a good chance of rolling over that IED if they hadn't.

It was a scary thought, and showed that no matter how good a job the clearance guys were doing, Daesh had gone all out to hide a hell of a lot of explosives along this route.

We were still in the middle of nowhere and despite this setback needed to get to the trapped soldiers. Standing out in the open was also making us easy targets.

'Leave the wreckage until later,' the Lieutenant ordered the men from the blown-up Humvee. 'Divide yourselves between the remaining vehicles and let's get back on the road.'

As we got close to the village I could see it was more of a hamlet, with a great deal of damage already done to the buildings by the airstrikes that night. There was a lot of gunfire coming from within the village, and stopping near a berm on the outskirts we dropped low and ran to join some Pesh already stationed there to take stock of the situation. Setting up our rifles we tracked the source of the gunfire into several buildings, and keeping low began returning fire.

As the firefight became heavier we were instructed to pull back, as some of the Pesh were still trapped in the village. We didn't want them to be caught up in the cross-fire. Despite the temptation to go all out, we needed to pause and assess. Watching and waiting was a tricky game, as we were lying down behind the berm and the sandbags, now totally exposed to the heat of the mid-afternoon sun and being eaten alive by the sandflies. But as standing up was asking to become a target, we had to put up with the bites, and keep watching.

Eventually the Lieutenant, who I was quickly learning was not a patient man, got sick of waiting and decided to go over the berm in one of the Humvees. He is hugely passionate about the fight, and vocal in his dislike of Daesh, but this attempt to push forward turned out to be a mistake. The ground had not been made as compact as normal and the vehicle got wedged on the top. Under incoming fire the boys were forced to dig it out. It was in too deep for shovels to make a difference, and each attempt put them at risk from the bullets whizzing past. Instead they used bits of old metal cable from fallen electric pylons, and with the help of a couple of carabiner clips from his rig, Baz was able to attach it to the MRAP and reverse that to pull the Humvee back over.

At the same time a soldier called Hajie who instantly earned himself the nickname 'Crazy Pesh' spotted another soldier stranded on the other side of the berm, rolling around moaning, clearly injured. Without a second thought he jumped over, attached a rope to him, and pulled him back to safety, before calling over one of the medics to deal with him. The guy was pretty cool, if a bit nuts, and

Akam seemed to think highly of him, keeping him close by at all times. He was a huge Neanderthal of a man who reminded me of the cartoon character Captain Caveman – particularly striking amongst the slight Kurds – and I came to think highly of him over time. He was well known locally for his track record of killing Daesh, and I was definitely someone I would want on my side, rather than against me!

The Lieutenant got a call asking our group to go further round the village to provide cover there, and again as we pulled up and ran low to set up behind the berm. Gunfire was coming out of the few buildings that were still standing, and we were forced to return. It was mainly small-arms fire – AKs, and the odd G3 rifle. It was tricky though, as we rarely actually saw the enemy and had to aim for the general area where the shooting was coming from.

Then a shout came through on the comms for help with injured Pesh. A couple of men had been really badly injured by IEDs and were already being treated, but two others with damaged legs were brought over to our vehicles for treatment. We had two medics on our team – Baz and one of the Americans, Kyle, who were both trained combat medics from back in their military days – but everyone tried to do what they could to help. The first guy was screaming and swearing so badly I was genuinely concerned about what we were going to see of his leg when the clothes were removed. Kyle laid the guy down and went to cut his trousers off to see what he was dealing with.

'No, they are my best trousers!' the man shouted, waving him away. I had to laugh. Clearly not so badly injured after all, then. Kyle rolled up the trouser leg instead, and discovered that luckily, despite the blood, the guy only had a superficial injury, so he bandaged him up and sent him on. Kyle was a great medic, and Baz was good at the job too, although funnily he always seemed to get the butt injuries. He was forever complaining that if anyone came to him for help, it always seemed to be something like shrapnel in their bum cheek that needed to be removed.

We started setting up the second guy for treatment on his leg and were totally focused on him, when the roar of an engine caused us all to turn. There was a car accelerating around thirty metres away, the pedal pushed to the floor so hard that the wheels were skidding, leaving a huge dust cloud in their wake. Three Daesh members clearly realizing it was their last chance to escape. Everyone around our vehicles dived for their weapons and opened fire, magazine after magazine exploding into the air, maybe a thousand rounds pumping out in the direction of the car. But we were just too late. Maybe some damage was done, but they were able to get off into the distance – weapons like AKs are only accurate to around three hundred metres. They were just that bit out of range before the shots began, but people were so angry and frustrated that they just kept on firing. The Pesh wanted these fuckers dead so badly.

Then it all went quiet, as though that fleeing car had taken the last remaining live Daesh in the village. The SP – Standard Procedure – is to make sure the village is clear, so we split into groups to search. At the same time we kept an eye out for anything that Daesh had left behind that could be of use to us – not just weapons or ammo but also things like Calor-gas canisters, which went for thirty bucks down the market. Even the odd bit of household equipment was helpful to add to our compound. This particular trip we got fifteen gas canisters, a fridge, an air-con unit and a few bits of ammo, which filled the vehicles to capacity.

Then we headed off so that the bulldozer teams could come in and raze the village to the ground. I questioned the reason for this, and was told it was so there was nothing left for Daesh to come back to. 'What about when the people return who lived there originally?' I asked, but I was told by the locals that no one ever wanted to come back to a home that had been inhabited and sullied by the enemy. They would rather build again from scratch. Besides, the village was pretty much destroyed by then anyway.

Then we headed back to the road, with plans to collect the injured Humvee en route to our compound. Unlike the UK, when going over a speed bump can see your car classed as written off, out here we tried to salvage vehicles, especially when they were worth hundreds of thousands of pounds. We were to tow it back to the compound and see what could be done.

'Whoa, whoa, whoa!' came shouts from ahead, as we reached the road. 'They've found another IED. Stay back!'

'This is the road we came down on the way!' I thought, shaken. 'Strange that a matter of a few inches in your driving can potentially save your life.' I settled on the ground to wait, contemplating our luck. Out of all the vehicles we had, our MRAP was the safest to be in if you were to go over one of those things, but still . . .

As it turned out, the mine-clearing team found another ten IEDs on that stretch of road. Over the next two hours we sat there while they blew them up, feeling more and more thankful to have survived with each controlled explosion. Each time one went off, I would think how that could have been the end of us.

The roadside bombs used here were created by burying a charge at the side of the road, with a metal strip running across the road, buried under the soil, with a u-bend in it. A piece of wood was put above the bend with a nail sticking in it, and if someone drove over the wood it pushed the nail down to complete the circuit, and boom, the IED blew up.

We finally got back to the compound at 19:00, a good twenty-four hours after we set out on the mission. I was tired, but happy that we had been able to achieve something, that we had helped rescue trapped Pesh, deal with injured fighters, and get rid of Daesh from that village. One more area cleared of their evil.

The Sheikh's top guys had us over to the house for dinner to say thank you for the help, which was a nice gesture, and allowed us to bond a bit more with the Pesh guys as well. Nothing like going through firefights and surviving IEDs to draw a group of men closer!

A few days later a couple of Welsh guys contacted IDET from Erbil. They wanted to join, but were making all sorts of outrageous claims, so Rupert sent Tyler, plus Baz and me, to meet them, saying: 'I don't always understand the Brits and how their minds work, at least you two can suss them out.'

We met in TGIs in Erbil, and instantly I was unimpressed – one of them was so fat and out of shape, he struggled to get into his seat. Then they were off, talking arrogantly, as though they were vetting us, rather than the other way around. One of them claimed to have twenty-five Black Hawk helicopters that could be put to use as transports, and was talking about people getting paid $450 a day to be there, rather than it being voluntary. When I asked if they had been to Kurdistan before, one of them kept saying: 'Loads of times, mate, always to Baghdad.' Hmm, if that was his knowledge of geography, I was unsure.

I made a few calls, and found out they had a small security company in South Wales, but none of the equipment they claimed.

'We could get them down anyway,' I said to Baz, 'just for a couple of days' trial. You never know if they might come good, as at least they have security background, and either way it could be entertaining!'

So we told them to meet us at the hotel the next day and we would take them back to the compound. An hour before the agreed meet-up time we got a text. 'IDET is not what we really want to do actually, I think we want to go in a different direction.'

That different direction, as I later discovered, was out of Kurdistan. Yet more people who had turned up for the visit and the photos, to add to their website – no doubt to try and give some credibility to their security company – and once they had that and the ego boost it gave them, they were out of the country faster than their fat little legs could take them. Clearly Dwekh wasn't the only group that suffered from wannabe volunteers wasting their time.

12

THE QUICK REACTION FORCE

For the next couple of weeks we sat on our beds, waiting. I realized I was not very good at the downtime thing, and the reality of war is that there is a lot of it. The exciting, adrenalin-filled moments are not as common as I had thought they would be. Despite being told repeatedly by the others who had done time in the military that this was normal – 'hurry up and wait' was the way they described the lifestyle – I did find it tricky.

I had brought several hard drives full of films, and I spent a lot of time watching them to pass the time. Or I would play with Ollie and take him for walks. I don't think I could have made my equipment any cleaner and more gleaming, inside and out, if I tried. I also made the most of our makeshift gym, but ultimately I was bored.

Eventually it became clear that it would be like this for a few weeks as the Sheikh was away on business, so we were unlikely to get orders to push forward until he returned. So rather than wait any more, I decided to head over to Duhok for a couple of days and then on to Baqofa to see the boys, especially JP, who still had the hump with me for deserting him.

I figured it would be a couple of weeks until action in IDET picked up again, so I could stick with Dwekh temporarily and see if there was any action there. A few days later I was back at the front in Baqofa, standing on the roof of the Dwekh house, watching mortar rounds incoming, as though I had never been away. JP got hold of an explosive that had fallen nearby and turned it into a footrest while he sat on the roof, in a message of defiance that we were not afraid of anything Daesh sent our way.

We also made a video of JP and me trying to sing a traditional Assyrian song, taught to us by one of the locals. We really struggled to pronounce the words and had no idea what we were actually saying, although I was told it was a love song, but it was great fun, and had us in stitches. When I posted it online it seemed to hit a nerve with people, and was viewed tens of thousands of times within days, and shared on Assyrian websites with people calling it 'Assyrian X Factor'. Viewers were laughing at our dreadful attempt, but complimenting us for trying to embrace the culture as well as just being there to fight. It was a good bonding moment!

We also called into the General's house to say hello. He wasn't there, but we came across a Western friend who was now working directly with the Peshmerga. It was a great sign that Western volunteers were being taken more seriously by the Kurdish army.

But it seemed I had got lucky for those initial few days, and that the fear of anything happening to us had escalated. Absolutely no one seemed to be able to get us the right permissions to be at the front line. Manny was in America fundraising for Dwekh and raising awareness of the plight of his people, so was not able to help, and Ahmed had moved on. Instead our only point of contact was a guy called Bahir, who was tasked with raising the profile of the group. His head was in the clouds, though, and nice though he was, he was no use in this area.

Marcus and the others were still around, but they didn't really have any sway over what we were allowed to do. Besides, they were all trying to plot their way out of the country and on to a new life, knowing that this war didn't look like it would be ending any time soon. Marcus told me it was his dream to emigrate to Canada, and I felt sad for him as I wasn't sure it would ever happen. He had been working hard to develop a women's shoe shop he had set up in Duhok, and he was very focused on getting a better quality of life. It seemed unfair that just because of where he was born he was unlikely ever to get the opportunity to take his well-meaning and business-minded self to Canada. It made me realize how lucky I was to be born in a country that on the whole is peaceful, united, and offers plenty of opportunity to expand on your life.

Frustratingly, a few days after I arrived there was a huge offensive at the Baqofa front, with incoming fire from

Daesh in Batnaya ramping up a level, and much heavier than usual, but we were told they couldn't let the Westerners take part in any retaliation. I stormed down to Bahir the next morning, and asked, 'What time do you want us here tonight? I assume after last night you need everyone holding the line that you can get?'

'I can't let you down there, I am sorry. We can't get the permission because we are Christians, I am sorry.'

'Rubbish!' I exploded. 'You are all playing at being soldiers, you are just worried you might actually have to get on with doing some real work on the front if we came down. Do you want to deal with Daesh or not?'

He just shrugged and kept apologizing, blaming everyone else. I lost my rag, and ranted to JP about their incompetency.

'I accept there is a lot of waiting around,' he said, equally frustrated, 'but when there is something happening where we could be put to use, it becomes a bit of a fucking joke.'

It was now December, and I decided to get back over to Kirkuk, as things were due to be picking up again.

I had been gutted not to have JP with me over there, and we had a long chat about where we would be most useful in helping the cause. That one day on the front in IDET, plus everything the boys had told me about previous missions they had been on, meant as far as I was concerned it did seem to have the most potential. Eventually

JP decided that he had stuck it out at Dwekh for long enough hoping the action would improve, and agreed it would be best if he came along with me. He was still far and away the best person I had worked alongside in Baqofa, and I believe he felt the same thing about me. At times I think we felt like the most normal level-headed volunteers out there. I knew he had my back 100 per cent and vice versa, and it wasn't just a working relationship, he had become one of my best friends. You see a person's true colours in front-line situations, and the trust and understanding we had developed was second to none.

Baz came over to see us in Duhok and to meet JP. Ironically JP had nearly joined IDET when he had initially looked to go out to Kurdistan, but had come over to Dwekh at the last minute. Because of previous conversations he had had with the group, his military background, and my high opinion of him, the guys were more than happy to have him on board.

At the same time, Baz told us that I wasn't the only one who had been frustrated when things had begun to wind down in Kirkuk, and that a lot of the Americans had left, including Rupert, taking the dogs Rose and Charlie with them. I was sorry to see them leave after enjoying my first mission with them, but was pleased to hear Baz had been told there was more action on the horizon for IDET and Westerners were to be more involved alongside the Peshmerga.

Before we left Duhok, we bumped into some French guys we had previously fought alongside, who had also moved over to working with the Peshmerga. The Paris attacks had happened earlier that month on 13 November, when a series of coordinated suicide bombings and mass shootings had taken place leading to the deaths of a hundred and thirty people. We briefly touched on the issue. They were upset about it, but ultimately they were out doing something about it.

I had been horrified by the images and the stories of what all the poor people had gone through, particularly at the concert in the Bataclan, where the terrorists had carried out a full-blown massacre. But sadly, I wasn't actually surprised by the events. As I had said when there were the beach attacks in Tunisia, I was expecting Daesh to start more of these targeted attacks against the West, each carried out by just a handful of people.

Straight after the Paris attacks I was inundated on Facebook with messages from French people, some wanting to donate to the cause, others keen to come out and join. There was a lot of anger about the atrocities, as well as a lot of patriotic statements that their country wouldn't be bullied like that, and I was pleased to see so many people kicking back.

But then it all faded as fast as it had begun. Within a few weeks all the motivation and frustration abated, and the promised hordes of volunteers never materialized. It was a real eye-opener for me, and left me hugely disappointed. People wanted to express their outrage, but changing their Facebook profile picture to having a French flag over it or ranting about it in the pub is as far as it went. People like feeling outraged, and then that venting is all they need for their anger to dissipate, before they turn back to normal life. People were too worried about upsetting the odd person, or coming across as unsympathetic to the plight of the enemy, so they would let it go. But for me that was the one way to ensure it would happen again. I was adamant that sadly Paris was not going to be a one-off.

As for the locals in Kurdistan, they registered what had happened in Paris, but it wasn't hugely on their radar. They were understandably more concerned with their own daily battle with Daesh. In the way that in the UK so many people see problems in the Middle East as issues belonging to another world, the same can be said in reverse. There was sympathy for the Parisians' plight, but they had their own much worse version of it to deal with.

At the same time, I had been following the debate and then vote over airstrikes in Syria by the UK government and was glad when it went through. Although it was a drop in the ocean of what I believed needed to be done, it was at least a start.

We headed over to IDET in early December, and as Baz had said, several of the group had left, reducing us down to six – us three, Kidd, and two Americans called Chris and Ash – but it felt like a tight group of people who were there for the right reasons, with no bullshit. We were officially given the title of QRF (Quick Reaction Force), ready for action at all times to support the Peshmerga. We decided to recruit for more volunteers, but this time they would be closely vetted! Basic criteria were: 'Previous military experience. Physically fit. Of sound mind. Team player. Under 40. Available for a minimum of three months.' We were open to variations, as my own lack of military experience showed, as well as the fact a couple of the lads were in their forties, but at least we hoped that would help us hone in on good people. I didn't get too involved in recruiting, though. I have always been keen to educate and provide information, but feel that people need to decide to come of their own volition. Besides, I found it embarrassing telling people not to come if they weren't ex-military as I couldn't blame them if it rubbed them up the wrong way coming from me.

One of the huge differences for me in working with IDET versus Dwekh was that they were much more closely affiliated with the Peshmerga, so the set-up was much more professional, and crucially, we were not expected to fund ourselves to the same degree. Weapons and ammunition were provided, and we were fed – key things for soldiers who might be out there indefinitely, but with a finite amount of money! It was also useful in that it meant recruiting could be opened up to people with less money behind them.

Having said all this, the food left something to be desired. Meals were in the mess, one of the prefab buildings that had been designated for that purpose. The menu always seemed to be red shit and rice, green shit and rice, or yellow shit and rice . . . I am told they were supposed to be soups based on tomatoes, cucumber or chickpeas, but they were vile. The cucumbers didn't look like my idea of a cucumber, and the chickpeas were the worst, but it was all they ate! Apart from the one day a week that is, when we were lucky enough to get chicken with the rice. Often I would just get one of the boys to bring me back a plate of rice and I would add something from my own stock to it, to mix it up a bit and get some variety. I kept boxes of food in the house that had been sent out from the UK, or I would buy supplies on the odd shopping trip such as chicken burgers or patties. I would get two hundred at a time and keep them in a small freezer. The boys would come up and buy them off me, putting their dinars on the bed, and saying, 'How many burgers do I get for this?' I always sold them for cost price, mind, it was just a way of making life more pleasant, I wasn't trying to run my own business on the side.

There were also sweet treats in my boxes that I had sent out myself, or that supporters had sent to give us a boost. The party ring biscuits were my favourite. Retro!

One night Baz brought a chicken doner back to the room for me while I was in the gym so afterwards I needed to heat it up. We had no facilities, so I was trying to do it by resting my plate on top of the electric heater. It was daft, and I decided it was about time I got my own one-ring hob for the room from Kirkuk, but I needed the help of the Peshmerga for that.

We didn't mix too much with the Peshmerga, for two

main reasons. There was the key issue of the language barrier, but also because on the whole they didn't like dogs, and we had gathered quite a motley selection by then. As well as Ollie, who was growing bigger by the day, we had Baz's dog Max, and several other strays who came and went when they needed food and attention. The Pesh couldn't see why we would have any interest in the dogs, and they regarded them with a mixture of disgust and fear. It was a mutual feeling, though; the dogs didn't like the Kurds and would get restless or growl if they came near. I guess they knew that they were more likely to get a kick or a whack from a Kurd, whereas it was all food and pats from the Westerners!

But we got on well with a few of the Peshmerga who could actually speak good English, and a couple of these guys agreed to take us into Kirkuk to get what we needed. Kirkuk is a beautiful old place, based in and around the citadel, which makes up the oldest part of the city. It is about eighty-five kilometres south of Erbil, and is one of the southernmost cities, before you move out of Kurdistan and into Iraq.

Kirkuk has switched hands dozens of times over the years, not least I am sure because of its huge oil riches. It is in the biggest oil-producing region in the country, which makes up nearly half of Iraq's oil exports. The population of close to one million is believed to be majority Kurds, initially due to them moving to the area to work in oil and living in previously uninhabited rural areas on the outskirts of the city. Ethnic cleansing of the city from the 1970s onwards saw attempts to remove them out of the area, but in the aftermath of the war with Saddam, they returned en masse.

The city was under the rule of the Iraqi government, but when the Iraqi Security Forces fled the north of the country, giving up the fight with Daesh, and the Peshmerga continued the fight alone, the Kurds also laid claim to Kirkuk. So it was presently under the rule of the Kurdistan Regional Government, although because it contained other peoples – in particular Arabs and Turkmen – it had a somewhat unsettled feel to it. I am told there is due to be a referendum on its future, but I would like to see it gain some stability as part of Kurdistan. It would also be great for the Kurds, who aren't a particularly well-off people, to have a decent source of income from the Kirkuk oil.

As we walked around the town it was fascinating to see so many old historical areas and some really quite striking and beautiful buildings. But the shopping was not proving so easy on the eye, with the prices charged and being haggled over becoming more ridiculous by the minute. One item I wanted had cost me $38 in Duhok brand new, and in Kirkuk, it was clear I had my work cut out when I was asked for $200 for a second-hand version!

It didn't have the relaxed atmosphere of Erbil either. The general feeling was more hostile, and it was clear it was not so liberal, with many of the women walking around covered up, with everyone going about their business, and less noise and chatting in the streets.

At the same time I was very aware that we were getting a lot of stares. I wasn't too happy about how vulnerable we felt, even though we had come well-armed, having been warned that the risk of kidnap or attack by Daesh was high. There was a strange tense vibe, and we tried not to stay in any one place for too long. At moments like that you realize that you really are out there solo and very alone, and that you need to have complete trust in the people you are with.

Eventually we headed back to base – bizarrely passing a human leg on the way, in the middle of the road. There was still a boot on the foot and a ripped piece of trouser on the leg, with the open fleshy wound sticking out the top. It was pretty gruesome, but people were just driving around it without a second glance, as though it was something as basic as a pothole that needed avoiding. I have no idea why it was there in the middle of the town, but again it was part of the 'life is cheap' attitude that existed out there. The daily death toll meant that something as simple as a leg in the road was not an issue to get upset about. It was self-preservation from going crazy, on a mass scale I suppose – or just simply that they had become immune to it.

On the upside of that trip anyhow, I now had my hob, and made pasta and tuna for dinner that night. Such a simple meal, but so, so good . . . . As it wasn't yellow shit and rice!

*

It was now coming up to Christmas and tension was growing. It was felt that the traditional day of celebration for Christians would be a likely time for an attack by Daesh. Christians in the area pushed ahead with celebrations and plans, putting up Christmas trees, and Merry Christmas signs in their windows despite a warning from Daesh that anyone participating in the celebrations, or even acknowledging their existence, would be severely punished. I felt proud that so many local people were not put off their way of life, and were cracking on with their Christmas plans.

We started thinking of ways we could celebrate a Christmas of sorts, and I did my best to make myself feel festive and even more at home by putting up my favourite Cheryl Cole poster! I had brought it out especially, and the others were quite clearly jealous they hadn't thought to do the same. Instead they had to make do in other ways. Flags were a popular choice to hang, and JP had a tea towel with a dictionary of Scottish phrases on it that he proudly pinned above his bed, not that it helped any of us understand him any better. People had photos of their family out there too, but for security reasons these were tucked away, and not put out on general display.

We got hold of some Santa hats, and discussed whether we could do ourselves a Christmas lunch, or give gifts. On 23 December I was contemplating wrapping up an ammo pouch for a Secret Santa present when we suddenly got word that we should prepare ourselves for a Christmas Eve mission. It turned out that we weren't going to wait for Daesh to come to us, we were going to them. This was the kind of Christmas present I was really after! I got stuck into preparing my kit, and could hardly sleep for excitement about the next day.

The six of us were up and good to go at 7:00 on the 24th, but the Pesh were far from ready, so I tried to get a bit more head-down time, lying on my bed in full kit. I've always been a good timekeeper, so if someone says a time I will be ready on the dot, but it is not so out here. People joke about Caribbean timekeeping, but I can say that Kurdish timekeeping is not much better!

Two hours later we set off and drove to a camp at the front line, where for several hours we were put on duty to provide cover for some Special Forces guys from NATO countries. At this time no government was admitting to having 'boots on the ground' but there were obviously some who were sending small teams to help, and for intelligence-gathering. This day we were working with one of these, who were there to observe this particular front line, to work out what airstrikes would be called in in the near future, and to monitor the results of several drones. We had seen people who were clearly from foreign forces on several occasions both in Baqofa and now in Kirkuk, but generally there was no mixing, and I didn't feel it was my place to ask anything. They would often use drones, but what info they gathered, or what they were able to do with that, I am unsure, and for security reasons it would have been inappropriate to ask. The encampment was based by an old railway track that was no longer in use as

it ran between allied territory and that being commandeered by Daesh. We explored that and the surrounding
area, looking for any potential threats, and keeping an eye
out. It was a good day to be out, and we enjoyed the gor-
geous sunny weather. In the winter months it is freezing at
night but the daytime, although still cold, is often bright,
sunny and clear. There is snow in the winter in Kurdistan,
but it tends to be more up in the mountains at high
altitude. So it was unlikely we would be getting a white
Christmas, but I could settle for that kind of perfect winter
morning.

Then another of those ridiculously surreal front-line
moments happened – a school bus pulled up. As the doors
opened we watched in disbelief as a crowd of fifteen-year-
olds bundled off the bus, jostling and chatting, as though
on a day trip.

The six of us stared in stunned silence at the group, as
their teacher walked them up to the high area that worked
as a good lookout point by the berm, where they were
greeted by one of the Peshmerga. He was obviously expecting them, and gave a ten-minute talk, pointing out key
areas on the horizon and giving them what looked like a
history, geography and politics lesson all in one.

Then the class, which appeared to be all boys, were
herded back on the bus and we watched as they drove off
down the front line, perhaps heading for the next stop
point to get another take on the war taking place in their
country. As they disappeared over the horizon, we turned

to look at each other and all burst out laughing. I have never seen anything like it in my life.

'Can you imagine the consent forms that went home to their parents?' snorted JP. '£2.50 to cover the cost of little Johnny's lunch, oh and could you sign here to say you accept there is a high risk of death on this trip, and the school will not be held responsible.'

We couldn't stop laughing. Of all the weird and wonderful scenes we had seen on the front line, this took the prize. I had long accepted that for the Kurds war had become part of everyday life, and they just got on with it, but . . . this?!

I wondered too what the kids had taken away from it. It had looked like a typical school outing anywhere, with some pupils listening attentively, others staring bored into the distance, and a few messing around and not paying any attention. Did they realize that their futures could be entirely determined by the outcome of this war?

After a bit more patrolling, the chow wagon turned up with the day's chicken and rice servings, then the Lieutenant asked everyone: 'Do you want some fun? There is a nearby river, which is horrible and polluted, with all sorts of rubbish and scum floating in it. If anyone will swim in that for ten minutes, I will pay you each fifty bucks!'

'This is a pretty easy day on the front,' I commented, wondering if anyone would take him up on the challenge. But just as the words were out of my mouth, the Lieutenant got bored, and decided the fun was over, and it was time for the work to begin. 'Time to clear the villages!' he shouted, and signalled us over the berm.

Instantly alert, the six of us Westerners plus half a dozen of the Pesh soldiers jumped over the trench and set off on foot patrol to inspect three villages that had been taken by Daesh, but recently recaptured by the Peshmerga. There had been an airstrike a couple of days before, and it was believed all Daesh had been killed or escaped but no one had actually pushed forward to check it out. The foreign teams were not allowed to, and the Pesh holding that line hadn't wanted to. So it was our job to check that there were no Daesh remaining in the villages or attempting to return there. Once we gave it the all-clear, the villages would be destroyed, then the area would become a sort of no-man's-land. The fortifications of the front line are so entrenched it is hard to physically move them with each village recaptured but if Daesh are prevented from returning it is a success.

We walked into no-man's-land on full alert, spread five to ten metres apart, patrolling with our rifles raised. It was flat, open land, and we were aware how exposed and vulnerable we were, so were on high alert, observing every dip in the ground just in front of us, through to watching out for any shimmer of movement on the far horizon.

It was rough terrain, consisting mainly of rough dirt fields with deserted crops still trying to push their way through the ground, despite no one looking after them any longer.

After fifteen minutes we arrived at our first village, and

found it had been completely annihilated, and was now mostly just piles of rubble and twisted metal spikes. We split up and looked around the mess, finding evidence of life in the abandoned clothing and blankets, and dirty blue makeshift curtains still blowing in the wind, but it was clear there was no one here. Chris and Ash took up positions on the roof of one of the few buildings still standing, so that they could get a clear view of the surrounding area and cover us as we headed on to the next village. There was a concrete irrigation ditch four metres wide and two metres deep that we needed to cross on the way that flagged as an obstacle that would leave us exposed, but we got across it, pulling Baz along with us, who was struggling in the heat. In the next village shell cases everywhere showed there had been heavy fighting, but seeing it was all clear, we radioed through to Chris and Ash to join us.

We headed along the ditch to the third village, aware that the deeper we got into no-man's-land the closer we were to Daesh territory, and therefore the more likely we were to come under attack.

Suddenly a call came through from Pesh on the front line – they were keeping an eye on us with spotting scopes, and were under instruction to call us about any movement. 'Potential risk of a vehicle-borne IED on the horizon.' A VBIED is a car bomb driven at you by a suicide bomber, who detonates once close enough. They use knackered old trucks or cars, with steel plates welded to the front for protection so that the driver can get close enough to their target without being shot. Once he's where he wants to be, he will detonate it, blowing himself and the vehicle up, and causing as much damage as possible.

We looked around but there was no sign of an approaching vehicle. We kept an eye out, all senses on high alert while checking the village, where there were signs that people had been camping out recently, with more blankets and clothing lying around. There were no signs of life though, and it seemed the airstrike had done its job – it was definitely no longer a Daesh-run area. It was a good feeling to know that the enemy were being pushed back, and that they couldn't hold their ground. At the same time it was a shame that these villages had to be destroyed as part of the process. Pointless destruction because of these idiots and their ongoing campaign, that I was determined they would never win.

Then we spotted a tank partially hidden in a dip in the ground. Heading over it was clear it was an old Iraqi T-55 that had most probably been taken and used by Daesh, but had then been hit during an airstrike. It was damaged beyond repair and Baz took the number plates off it as a reminder. Just as we were about to leave, the Lieutenant spotted the back end of a smart bomb – a precision-guided missile – that had most likely been used to take out the Daesh position and tank. He waved me over.

'I want this. You can carry it back for me, big man.'

Oh great, another 10 kilos was just what I needed for the hike back, in case all my other kit wasn't heavy enough!

This was the last of the villages that had been attacked

– the next one that we could see, just one kilometre away, was still under Daesh control, black flags flapping in the wind. As I heaved the missile up onto my shoulder, the Lieutenant decided it was time to head back, and we started to make our way back to the front line. Mission completed.

Just as we arrived in the second village shots rang out around us. We dived for cover behind some crumbling walls as Dushka fire whizzed overhead. It was coming from the village that was still under Daesh control, and was potentially where our spotter had seen the vehicle driving around.

My adrenalin was instantly pumping, and turning to the guys I said: 'Chickens! They waited until we were walking away from them to open fire! They must be afraid. We have to go back now and engage. We will definitely take them out.'

But the Lieutenant was happy we had achieved what we were required to do, and decided we needed to return. So we cut through to the back of the village, and headed on to the front line with the ruined building acting as a shield. I did as instructed, but I was disappointed, and kept turning back to see if the Daesh fighters had the nerve to follow us. No such luck.

As we drove back to the compound in the dark a couple of hours later, the Lieutenant ordered us to slow down as we approached a checkpoint as there was a suspicious-looking car pulled up by it. I was half-asleep and frozen stiff with the cold. But I heard him shout something at the men in the car in Kurdish, and unintelligible yells came back. Whatever they said I have no idea, but the Lieutenant wasn't happy with it, and fired his rifle into the air as a warning shot. Suddenly bullets were flying around us, and I instinctively ducked. We were in a soft-skin 4x4 truck, so there was very little protection, and I heard the bullets ricocheting off the shield of the Dushka gun mounted on the back. They were thudding into the ground around the vehicle too which put me off jumping out. You would normally bail out in a situation such as that, as the vehicle is a magnet for the bullets, but instead JP and I dived for shelter behind the Dushka shield, readying our weapons for the Lieutenant's sign to return fire.

There was more shouting and the Lieutenant radioed frantically through to the checkpoint. Suddenly the firing stopped. It turned out it was Peshmerga firing on us. Yet another moment when we nearly got taken out by friendly fire, although to the locals incidents like that are more of an inconvenience than a big deal. At times I was sure there was a much higher risk of me dying from that, than at the hands of Daesh!

It was around 02:00 on Christmas Day by the time we got back to base. Exhausted, we got our kit back in order – no matter what, it always needed to be ready to use so that we could be in action at a moment's notice – then we all wished each other Merry Christmas and fell into bed, passing straight out.

*

The next day wasn't exactly like Christmas as I know it. I woke up freezing. Temperatures can drop to zero degrees overnight, and even my new leopard-print blanket was failing to do the trick. Then we just sat around chatting, bemoaning the lack of TV. The worst bit was the food . . . Our Christmas lunch was lentil soup, with some mouldy old flatbread. Yep, that was all we had. We tortured ourselves thinking of the turkey, stuffing, roast potatoes and lashings of gravy that everyone back home would be tucking into, and I felt a pang of sadness at missing out on the day with friends and family. I could picture them sat around enjoying dinner, then retiring to the lounge to watch the Queen's speech. I love my Queen, and always watch her speech, so I was gutted to miss her!

13

THE TIDE BEGINS TO TURN

After Christmas another fifty Peshmerga recruits arrived, and lined up outside the camp to get their kit and orders. I sat on a wall watching with JP and Ollie, and was glad to see the ranks swelling in size. These newbies took the number in Sheikh Jafar's compound up to around three hundred, making it a decent-sized unit.

Again it struck me how young and innocent so many of them looked, and JP and I went over to give them a hand sorting their kit and straightening their Pesh patches, as the youngest ones always seemed to have them at odd angles. The key thing though was helping get their vests in order, as they rarely seemed to put them together properly, and they were of such cheap quality they needed a lot of remedial work, not to mention a word or two of advice on the contents. Hardly any of them seemed to have the basics they would need. JP even found a bottle of after-shave in one lad's pouches. He pulled it out, tucked a field dressing in its place, patted the kid on the shoulder and commented: 'I think you'll find that's more useful on the front line, mate.'

The recruits would be put through a couple of weeks of drill and basic training, and we'd see them being run around the camp and screamed at, but after that they were straight out into the field.

The battle against Daesh felt as though it was going in the right direction at the end of 2015, as though the tide was beginning to turn against the enemy. They were far from defeated, but it did seem as though they were in retreat. The towns of Tikrit, Baiji and Sinjar had all been retaken by Pesh soldiers, and now the key city of Ramadi, which Daesh had controlled for the last seven months, had been taken back by the allies. It was considered a particularly important victory as Ramadi had fallen to the enemy in May 2015 mainly because Iraqi security forces had abandoned it. Coming hot on the heels of the fall of Mosul, the Iraqi people saw their military as corrupt and unwilling to fight. The retaking of Ramadi showed that the Iraqi army were capable of holding their own. They had air support from America, and there was Shia militia involvement on a small scale, but the majority of the ground work was carried out by Iraqis. From what I could gather, it went some way to restoring a bit of the faith in them that had been lost.

The help provided by the Shia militias was difficult on a political and moral level. Shia militias are privately funded armies that were mainly created during Saddam

Hussein's reign to fight for the rights of the Shi'ite people in what was then a Sunni-led regime. After the fall of Saddam the new government was mainly Shi'ite, but the militias continued to exist, often fighting for the government or alongside its forces, despite the fact that there have been international calls for them to be disbanded. In recent years they have been accused of corruption, frequent sectarian attacks and murders.

In the last year or so, the Shia militias played an important part in certain areas in the fight against Daesh, leading offensives in several key towns and cities, and gaining popularity. Ultimately, as I understood it, it was a case of 'the enemy of my enemy is my friend' – a common saying in Kurdistan. That is to say, as long as the Kurdish and Iraqi governments see Daesh as an enemy, and so do the Shia militias, there is peace between the groups. What will happen between them when this common enemy is squashed is going to be a big issue.

The rise of the Shia militias was a particular problem for the Peshmerga, as not only do the Shia militias dislike Sunni Muslims (which is the area of Islam that Daesh follow), they hate the Kurds with a passion. The majority of Kurds are Sunni Muslims, but there are many other religions practised by Kurds, including Shia Islam, Sufism, Christianity and Yazidism. Many of the militia actually work on the belief the Kurdish people need to be wiped out. Not something you want to hear from forces that are, theoretically, on your side.

Kirkuk, with its unstable set-up and Kurd-heavy presence, was proving to be a popular place for the existence of various Shia militias. If we were in the town we would often see them driving around, dressed in blue camouflage similar to that of the US Navy. I always thought it was a bizarre uniform choice given the country is pretty much entirely landlocked. We never had any direct contact, though.

With so many groups in the area, it wasn't always clear which local attacks were carried out by whom. For example, in December a couple of Christian graveyards were stormed in Kirkuk, with graves destroyed and desecrated as a protest at Christians being allowed to celebrate Christmas. It was believed to be carried out by a Shia militia, although no one knew for sure.

I still tried to avoid spending too much time trying to analyse the politics of the country, as there were so many groups and shifting loyalties that at times it seemed completely confused, bordering on nonsensical! But one evening I was told that a Peshmerga soldier from the base had been shot dead earlier that day. He was killed while manning a nearby checkpoint, and the shooter was a member of a Shia militia.

As usual I was told about it as a bit of news over a cup of chai, a piece of gossip to be dissected and passed on with curiosity rather than deep upset. I tried to find out why it had happened, but no one seemed to know much about it.

It was decided that nothing should be done while the

Sheikh was away. He'd gone to America to raise awareness of what was happening in Kurdistan and no one wanted to retaliate on something so delicate without his permission. It didn't stop the Westerners at IDET discussing the issues, though, and a lot of them were very concerned about what would happen after Daesh's defeat. There is no question that Daesh are the ultimate enemy, and the reason I went out there. But the more I learned about the politics and in-fighting in Iraq, the more it became apparent that the end of Daesh was never going to be the end of the conflict. There seemed to be innumerable groups all with their own petty grievances, small-minded religious demands or claims based on historic events from thousands of years before. And these groups were not prepared to compromise or to respect anyone else's way of doing things. It was effectively as though there was a huge culture of intolerance in the country, amongst not all, but many people.

There was even the possibility that the end of Daesh would just open up the way for another, even worse group to take their place. It sounds unimaginable that there could be such a thing – wasn't burning men in cages, raping and selling women as sex slaves, and carrying out acts of terrorism worldwide as low as people can get? I hoped so, but then many of us believed the Taliban were the worst kind of group there could be on the planet, and then Daesh emerged . . . The Taliban were beginning to look like a soft tolerant group in comparison. In fact they had even condemned some of the action of Daesh!

Think about it too much and you'd get overwhelmed. I always came back to the fact that Daesh were the enemy, and sorting them out was what we were here to do. What happened beyond that needed to be faced in its own time.

Partly because of lack of action in the Sheikh's absence, and partly because the Kurds seem to think Christmas and New Year are one and the same thing, we were given a few days off around 31 December to celebrate. Even Santa – Baba Noel – hats just have '2016' written on them, as though that is what they are created to celebrate.

JP, Baz and I headed to Erbil, while the other three decided they fancied a break in Suli, as Sulaymaniyah was known. Getting from Kirkuk to Erbil was always an easy trip – there is a main road running between the two, and the journey of around a hundred kilometres took two hours maximum. There were three checkpoints on the way, but when you were travelling south you were rarely stopped at them, just waved on through. The attitude of the guards was, 'If you're foolhardy enough to want to head towards Daesh territory, then on your head be it!' But travelling in the other direction, the journey was a different matter.

A Pesh soldier needed to drop us into Kirkuk to the Erbil garage – the only taxi office in town where you could get to the other city as the local taxis won't leave their town – and then we had to argue the price and about who was in your car. I knew the acceptable price was

40,000 dinars for the journey, so would haggle until I got to that, then it was a matter of insisting I, or whoever I was with, travelled alone. Everyone out there shares taxis to reduce the price and they couldn't understand why we didn't want to do the same. But there was no way I was driving through the middle of nowhere with people I didn't know, partly from a financial viewpoint – not wanting to have any of my kit stolen – but more importantly from a safety viewpoint. There was just no way to vet your co-passengers. Once on our way, we would be stopped and thoroughly searched at each checkpoint – boots opened, bags inspected, papers looked over, the lot. There was a much higher risk that someone heading north was on their way to create a problem, so if these searches at the checkpoints were able to act as a deterrent, I was happy to comply.

A few hours later we were sat in one of the fourteen screens at the Empire Cinema in the Family Mall Shopping Centre, munching nachos and popcorn, and watching *Star Wars Episode 7: The Force Awakens*. It felt strange to think we had recently been on the front line, not far from here. But it is that sense of Kurdish resilience, that life goes on no matter what Daesh do, that I like. I suppose it exists in every country at war – for example the Brits may have initially stayed home during World War II, but after a while, despite the air raids, they would be heading to the cinema regardless, gas masks in their hands.

We had a curry afterwards in a great place called Mumtaz Mahal that very generously does free food for any Westerners who are here to fight Daesh. Then we spent the next day or so running errands for the group around the city, before it was time to celebrate New Year's Eve! A couple in Erbil who were friends of a friend kindly invited us to stay with them. They looked after us really well and we got out the alcohol for the first time in a while. I didn't feel my resolution of not drinking in Kurdistan extended as far as Erbil, as it was a world away from the front line.

As the clock struck midnight and we welcomed in 2016, I reflected on my last year. Although on the previous New Year's Eve I knew what plans I had laid out for myself for 2015, I had no idea what would actually happen in Kurdistan. JP and I debated whether we would have still gone out if we had known what lay ahead, and tried to predict where we would be on New Year's Eve 2016. I honestly didn't have a clue! One minute I could see myself still fighting for the cause, although maybe in another country, then the next I would hope I was enjoying a peaceful life back in the UK and finding the right person to settle down with.

The next day we headed back to Kirkuk and met up with Kidd, Chris and Ash at the base, who were all refreshed after their break in Sulaymaniyah. They had a fourth person in tow with them, an American called Sean who had arrived at Sulaymaniyah Airport while they were there, ready to join our fight. He was an ex-marine, looked in good physical shape and I instantly felt like he was going to add to the group in a positive way. He was knowledgeable and gutsy, but also funny and a bit of a joker, so we instantly had a good laugh together.

The first week of January was pretty dull, just sitting around and effectively experiencing the downside of being a Quick Reaction Force. We had to be ready to go at any moment, be it for instant action, or missions that could last several days, but in the interim it really was a case of killing time. I got so bored one day that I even went and did a litter pick around the compound, just to be active and put myself to more use than lying on my bed watching films.

As part of being set up as the Quick Reaction Force, I was asked by the Lieutenant to be the group's gunner. This meant that I had control of the unit machine gun, a PKM, and had to carry it whenever we were out and about. PKMs are Russian-designed 7.62mm infantry-support weapons and are relatively common in Kurdistan, having been used there during the Iraq War. We had nicknamed ours 'the Egyptian' as that's where we thought this particular one came from, although we later found out it was Chinese. I liked having a more defined role but the gun was blooming heavy, and I decided the gym regime might need to be upped even more.

There was a shooting range to the side of the camp where we could go and practise with any of our weapons. On the whole the Americans tended to use this most. For them guns are a way of life and they seem to get a lot more genuine pleasure out of using them. For me, they are powerful impressive weapons, but it is their practical use and the fact they can kill Daesh or save my life that is their real appeal. But the Americans would be there for hours, shooting down the range and practising different techniques and poses. They had to use their own weapons and ammo, though – the Pesh would have seen it as a waste of expensive rounds and wouldn't have been happy if ammo they had supplied was being used.

One day the Lieutenant got hold of a small civilian-style drone, and they were messing around with that, seeing exactly what it was capable of. It did produce some really clear and interesting footage and seemed that it could be really beneficial, so we began looking at ways we could make use of it, as well as trying to get hold of one of our own to keep.

A couple more American recruits joined us over the next few days – an ex-marine called Ryan, who was a very cool, surfer kind of guy from Pennsylvania who had previously modelled for Abercrombie and Fitch, and a quieter lad called Ross, who was ex-US Army. We were now up to nine Westerners in total.

Then during the second week of January we got orders to be ready for a three-day mission setting off the next morning. I had a 120-litre Bergen that was packed and ready to go for situations where we would be out for a few days. In this were waterproofs, medical kit, spare clothes, food, a hexi stove (a small fold-up cooker), night-vision goggles, sleeping bag, solar chargers, backup batteries, extra ammo, a knife, a pair of pliers, a pack of cable ties, Paracord, extra water and when I had the space, creature comforts such as hand warmers. We rarely had to do too much walking with our packs, and they were in the vehicles most of the time, so it was no problem to take too much – I'd rather that than miss out on something I needed! The only time it was an issue was getting back up to the bedroom at base. I was in the top bedroom and the staircase was tiny and narrow, so sometimes when I was all kitted up, carrying everything I would take out on a day, plus my Bergen, I could hardly fit up the stairs.

When not in use, the pack would sit at the end of my bed alongside my personal weapons, although I have been known to have my AK even closer – actually in bed with me as I sleep! Everything in the room was so compact and there was so little space to keep anything that I was worried if I left it out of sight someone would move it. You never knew when there might be an attack in the middle of the night, and if I didn't know where my weapon was, that would be a problem. With that in mind, having it tucked in the side of my bed seemed the safest option.

The next morning we were up and out to a cloudy grey day, and jumped into the trucks along with around thirty Peshmerga, then drove half an hour to a point near the front line. As usual the driving was so bad I thought we might die before we even reached our location! I was glad I had my big pack to sit on in the back, rather than the hard truck bed.

We pulled up at one point and all jumped out of the trucks, while intel was gathered and calls made by the Lieutenant and his deputy. I looked around at the Peshmerga who had come on this trip. A lot of them were Pesh new soldiers who had arrived in the recent recruitment drive, many still in their teens. It made me nervous to see how many of them had their weapons switched to fully automatic, scanning the horizon for threats with their fingers hovering just over the trigger. I realized they were new, keen and most likely on edge, but that was when things tended to go wrong, so I told them all to 'safety' their weapons, move their fingers off the trigger and settle down! I also didn't like the way they would leave other weapons lying untended in the back of the trucks, and I had visions of more friendly fire incidents . . . No matter how green I had been when I came out to join the fight, I would never have made these basic mistakes. The irony was that they had probably been around rifles since they were youngsters, but because they had never actually been taught how to use them, they had all sorts of bad habits that were practically impossible for them to un-learn.

JP and I had started referring to these new young Pesh soldiers as 'the Ant Hill Mob' as they were always scurrying round in a little group, almost afraid to leave each other's sides. With the black uniform of the Pesh on, they looked like the Ant Hill Mob from *Wacky Races*.

But before anyone got shot in the leg by their own side, we were all ordered back to the trucks and moved to the front line, just a little to the west of the area where we had spent Christmas Eve. Looking over to the right I could see the first of the hamlets we had cleared on our patrol, and was pleased that it still looked empty – there had been no attempts by Daesh to retake it then.

Looking across from our front line, beyond the no-man's-land to the enemy line seven hundred metres away, I could see a small Daesh-occupied village just behind it, with the usual large black flags flying from the rooftops. Looking through the scope we could see Daesh movement, the small figures dressed in black as usual, and not seeming to be doing anything in particular. I am sure they must have known we were there, but they didn't seem concerned, or give any indication that they were getting ready to retaliate. It was time to take them out.

But as we began to get ourselves organized, I scanned the rest of the area, and spotted a couple of cars parked up in the no-man's-land between us off to the left with people sat around them. I flagged them up but one of the few Pesh soldiers who spoke passable English told me, 'It is a refugee family who have set up a camp there. They are living there for now, as they are escaping Daesh.'

'Why are they sat there, though, in the firing line?' I asked, amazed. 'Surely they should be safely over here!'

'We can't let them into this territory. We take food out to them and help them when we can, but if these people are allowed to come, then everyone will, and we cannot cope with it. We need to make their villages safe for them so they can return there instead.'

It struck me as ironic that they were worrying about the floodgates opening from all the villages across the enemy side if they allowed this family to cross. While we had been having debates about the immigration crisis back in Europe, they were suffering a similar dilemma on a smaller scale within their own country.

He did add however that once in a while a bus was sent out to the area to collect refugees to take them to a camp, so they would hopefully get looked after eventually.

There was also another group of refugees set up over to the right, near the first of the hamlets we had cleared on Christmas Eve. They hadn't been there on our previous visit, and we watched them through the scope for a bit, before Akam told Baz, 'Take your medical bag and go and see if they need any treatment.' He headed out cautiously on foot, along with a few Pesh soldiers, to see what could be done. He wasn't able to do too much, though, as his medical kit was for use in the field, put together to deal with major trauma, and not filled with cough medicine or antibiotics, which is what these people were more in need of. After the group returned, the Pesh soldiers decided to take some spare food from the chow wagon out to them. I think we were all bothered that they were stranded out there – not just men, but women and children too – but it wasn't for us to make any decisions on where they should be, or challenge the reasoning of those above us. It was the Kurds' country and we had to assume they knew the best way to handle it.

I asked why Daesh hadn't killed any of these people, and was told that it was definitely extremely risky for those refugees to be there, and if they returned to the Daesh side they would inevitably be killed, but while they were sat in no-man's-land, it suited Daesh to have them there to occasionally act as a human shield. As it happened, where we were stationed that day these people had nothing to worry about as they were not in our arcs of fire – perhaps one of the reasons this spot had been chosen by the Lieutenant.

We set up the heavy weapons, and along with JP, Sean and Baz, I was put to manning the SPG-9. Originally a Russian weapon, it is a 73mm tripod-mounted recoilless rifle. It fires rockets like the RPG, but whereas that can be carried and shot from the shoulder, this needs to be set up on the ground, or a similar flat surface. The SPG-9 was a squad weapon for us, meaning it is not one specific person's job to fire it, so the four of us worked on it together.

Ash went to set up four hundred metres along the front from us, putting a 60mm mortar into position – a lightish mortar that was the main type we had used to date. The others split themselves between helping him and taking on observation duty on the elevated position between us, which gave great clear views across to the enemy position, and was where the school children had stood that day while getting their talk on the history of the war.

Small charges would normally be used on the SPG-9 to

launch the rounds, but as we didn't have any suitable ones, we were told to use our truck battery to spark it. We removed it from the car and got set up. Yet another example that the Pesh didn't have the financial resources to provide all the correct equipment for war. So many of the weapons we were fighting with were unsuitable, or missing parts, or were complete but lacking ammunition. But while it was frustrating, it brought out the creative and inventive in people, and the determination not to let this stop us trying to achieve results was impressive at times.

So once the projectile was loaded into the SPG-9, we touched the firing wires to the battery and it fired. We lined it up to aim at the building where we could see Daesh milling around, and we believed six of them had gone inside. I had ear defenders on, and didn't realize quite how loudly I was shouting, 'Five, four, three, two, one!' before I touched the wires to the battery. Nothing happened. Twice it failed to fire and the others started laughing, mocking me for the way I had loudly introduced it, only for it to lead to an embarrassing lack of success. Sean, who was videoing, caught my frustration on camera as I swore, 'Come on, you cunt!' I wanted to get a direct hit on this building so badly, although deep down I knew I would be lucky – reading up on the weapon beforehand I had seen that they were hard to get accuracy on until you were skilled with them.

I tried again, and this time whispered my countdown, so if things went wrong, I would feel less daft, and this time we were in business. As the projectile launched with a huge bang, we could hear it travelling across the open space. The sound reverberated through the air much the way the noise of a jet plane follows behind, after the aircraft is out of sight. It was an agonizing couple of seconds' wait, until the sound of it reaching its target. Sean, who was watching it through the scope, announced, 'Perfect hit, bro!' just as a cloud of smoke and dust rose up from where the building once was. On target! Everyone cheered, and the other boys started trying to claim the hit as theirs, for their work in helping set it up. But I knew it was mine. I had taken out some Daesh scum. I sent a second projectile over aimed at the same building to be sure we had taken out all the occupants, and again it was right on point. Success.

I didn't feel anything towards the people I was killing. I had long since stopped seeing Daesh as human, so as far as any empathy for them, I may as well have been shooting rubber ducks at the fairground. I hadn't felt anything but hatred for them before I had arrived in the country, after seeing and hearing everything they were capable of, but my time with the Kurds, hearing their stories and seeing just a fraction of the damage these fanatics had done to the country, had solidified my feelings. Right at this moment, all I wanted was another go on the SPG-9 to see if I could take any more of them out.

It was clear they hadn't been expecting incoming at all, despite the fact they could have easily seen us if they had been keeping an eye out. We had taken them out before they were even able to return fire. Ash also fired a few mortars to destroy some of the other buildings and any occupants, and was successful in hitting his targets too.

At one point at the far side of the village we could see what looked like a Daesh member escaping on a pushbike, pedalling manically to escape. Other than him though there was no movement, so they were either all dead or hiding. It looked like our job here, at least, was done.

As we packed up and began moving off to the next job a call came through on the radio. There was a lot of angry chatter back and forth between the Lieutenant and someone else, and suddenly he changed his mind about going onwards. It turned out someone had lost a weapon and for whatever reason he was particularly unhappy about this, so he shouted his orders and we all turned back to base. I was disappointed to be wrapping up so early on what I had been beginning to see as three potentially successful days, but I was happy with the day's work. Firing the SPG-9 and taking out a fair few of the enemy was a good feeling. It was extremely likely that in doing so we had saved the lives of civilians, perhaps even those refugees camped out nearby who seemed like sitting targets to me. While I wanted to get on and do more, I was pleased that I had done my bit.

Back at camp I took a ribbing for my very southern English accent, with the Americans and even some of the Pesh going round shouting, 'Come on, you cunts!' every time they passed me. If there was ever a downside to having your military actions – and errors – recorded on film, I was feeling it at this time!

I have to say, I hate hearing my own voice played back to me, and it does often get commented on. I even got called 'Squeak' for a while out in IDET, as they said my voice doesn't match my persona, something I hear a lot. When people see this big guy, they expect me to speak in a deep cockney voice or something. I'm not always high-pitched, by the way, only when I get animated or worked up about something.

JP once said, 'I saw pictures of you before I met you and did not expect you to sound like you do. When I heard you in person, I was like who the fuck is this?!' He was only saying that because he has a deep throaty Scottish accent, though.

To be honest I quite like the disconnect between my voice and appearance, as it throws people off. I had one guy recently even apologize for expecting me to talk like a Neanderthal before he had met me. I think it is ridiculous that people are that judgemental, but if I can prove them wrong, I will take the nickname Squeak in the meantime!

The day after our SPG-9 fun, word came through in the afternoon of enemy movement in no-man's-land and we went out again to that same section of the front line. We climbed out of the trucks and tucked in behind the berm, expecting a slow few hours, as there were often reported sightings, but they rarely seemed to amount to anything.

Not that we minded too much with yesterday having felt like a success. Akam was keeping an eye on everything through his scope, but wasn't picking anything out between us and the Daesh front line. Then he saw movement over in the village that we had fired on the day before, and decided it was worth some warning shots.

'Right,' he hissed quietly, 'fire five.'

I heard him and understood that he just wanted us to fire off five rounds, to send a 'fuck you, Daesh, we are here' kind of message, as we had no idea how many of them were over there or what they were up to. However, it seemed that a couple of the other lads hadn't quite got what he said. Instead they had understood it as an urgent request to 'Fire! Fire!' – that is to say, open up on them with everything you have got.

After so regularly being told to hold off, this was all the encouragement the boys needed and they were all up like uncoiled springs, weapons whipped over the top of the berm, opening fire for all they were worth into the ether in front of us. 'Fuck it,' I decided, caught up in the buzz of it, 'there is no way I'm not joining in with this!' I couldn't make out if there were actually people there, partly because of all the dust clouds we were creating, but at that moment I think we all imagined that there was a whole army of Daesh just out of sight, and we took immense pleasure in opening up on them. I think we were probably still on a bit of a high from the day before too, and wanted to continue on our roll of successfully taking out the enemy.

'Stop, you motherfuckers, stop!' Akam yelled, incensed. I saw JP look up in surprise, halfway through loading a second magazine into his rifle and totally convinced that he was doing as instructed. I couldn't stop laughing, partly I think from the adrenalin of the moment.

Akam was furious with us, but I thought it was worth it. It had been a chance for us all to unload our weapons, something it felt like we were always waiting for but rarely getting to do. Needless to say we were rapidly sent back to base, but all of us were in a lighter, jokier mood afterwards.

Back at the base we had another week or so of downtime. This meant a lot of washing, cleaning weapons, watching films and making use of the makeshift gym. I also did some bits of electrical work around the place. In these kinds of situation it is a case of making the most of your skills, and I knew I had the least military knowledge by a mile, but I was able to be useful in other ways too, and this was one of them. So simple things like rewiring, changing bust plugs and so on all fell to me.

JP and I also spent time teaching the Pesh how to play rugby. I had brought a couple of balls back with me from England as I thought it would be a good way to pass the time and some of the Pesh, as well as the Americans, were keen to try it. We marked out a bit of a pitch out the back of the compound, and taught them the rules, then we all got stuck in. It was the most ridiculously dangerous game

of rugby I have ever played. The Pesh did not really understand anything we had explained to them – or chose not
to, anyhow – so the rule book went out the window. It
turned into a mix of them trying to kick the ball like foot-
ball and then just running at us, turning it into an all-out
ruck, or 'thugball' as it became known. Not only that, but
the ground was completely inappropriate. There were
large sharp stones all over the place, and even bits of
barbed wire tucked into the earth that you wouldn't spot
until you were skidding towards them. It might be nothing
compared with the front-line risks, but there were a lot of
scraped, bruised and exhausted lads heading for bed that
night. Needless to say we struggled to get another game
together after they had seen what rugby 'the game of you
crazy Brits' was like.

It was a good bonding experience with the locals, as I
hadn't got to know these guys as well as those in Dwekh.
On the whole their English seemed to be worse for one
thing, but mainly it was down to the living arrangements.
Whereas in Duhok and Baqofa we were sharing a house,
and therefore day-to-day life with the locals, having our
own separate home here prevented that. We did have bits
of banter, but it was quite few and far between. I had to
laugh at one guy I'd given my spare knee pads to, as he
had liked the look of them. No one else on the camp had
any really, so once he put them on they never came off. He
would wear them constantly – at the front line, walking
around the camp, down to dinner . . . I liked that he was
so proud of them.

We also spent a lot of the downtime with the dogs. JP and I would walk Ollie and Max a couple of times a day in the area around the base, but there were also a fair few other dogs in the group by now. There was Foxy, who obviously looked like a fox, and had decided to join us one day, as well as a husky that one of the Pesh had bought, and then a day later gave to us, although he ran off soon after, and a small Pesh-owned dog that was just known as the wee yapper. He was often tied up to one of the vehicles outside, and whenever we walked our dogs he would yap away until we got near, then go quiet and meek until we had passed, then the barking would begin again, as he gave it the big 'I am'.

There was one other dog called Auto, who one of the lads had found on the front line one day and brought back, but he died soon after, showing signs of poisoning, although we had no idea who might have been responsible. Perhaps he ate something disgusting of his own accord. Ollie got sick another time and I was convinced that was because he had found something dead and rotten and eaten that, so maybe Auto had done the same.

Sadly there had been no news about Rocky. People at Dwekh were still under instruction to let me know if he ever reappeared, but I don't think he will. I just have to hope that he wasn't despatched with a 9mil but has found himself a new owner in the next village along who gave him a better life than he had with us!

Then there was the cat – Combat Kitty. She was part of the group before I arrived, having been rescued by one of the lads. They had been burning an area of scrubland behind the base to create a shooting range when he had heard some mewling and got the cat out of the under-growth. He had looked after her for a while but on his departure she had moved out and become feral. For what-ever reason she had now decided to move back inside. The dogs hated her and would bark and chase after her, but she was always too quick for them, and perhaps because of them, spent much of her time living in the rafters. Before her return JP had regularly complained about the noisy birds on the roof in the morning. Now Combat Kitty was there they had disappeared, but instead she was forever scratching about, and even jumped down your back and shoulders if you went to the loo in the middle of the night. I was less than amused. I would always take a plate of something up when I went for a shower and set it on the shelf above my head for her to get stuck into.

One afternoon I was in the gym when a soldier came run-ning in to say I was needed in the guard room, as two spies had been caught. It turned out that one of the guys who worked in the kitchens had invited a mate onto the base, and in true Kurdish style they had been taking selfies all over the place. But then suspicions were aroused as they were no longer just photographing themselves, but seeming to document all the vehicles, taking pictures from all angles. When confronted they had become cagey, and were hauled in front of Akam to explain themselves. As I arrived one of them tried to take a swing at the Lieutenant, so I jumped in and restrained him. The two had their phones removed and were questioned while Crazy Pesh had rocked up and was leaping around nearby, desperate to get his hands on them! Being so patriotic and committed to the cause, he was furious that these two had potentially been spying for the enemy, and was enthused at the idea of teaching them a lesson. Eventually we were told to shave their heads and put them into the cells. They were later handed over to Asayesh for them to determine any guilt or punishment, although I never heard the outcome. It was concerning that not everyone on base might be as committed to the cause as the rest of us.

Around this time I was contacted by a television producer who told me he worked with Ross Kemp and was scouting for locations to shoot with him in Iraq, and that he had been passed my details by another Western volunteer. He was keen to bring Ross down to IDET to spend some time with us, interview the boys and see what day-to-day life was like.

Although I'd never met Ross, I had seen some of his previous series, in which he had visited various gangs around the world as well as several front lines, and he had always seemed a decent enough guy. I enjoyed the shows and he did a good job of highlighting things happening around the world. It is always hard to know what has gone on behind the scenes with documentaries such as these though, so I was keen to meet up with the producer before making any commitments on behalf of the rest of the boys. I wanted to hear about what was required, and what say we would have over keeping certain people's identities hidden and so on.

He told me when he was planning to be in Erbil, and I agreed to head up for a few days. Baz pulled me to one side and said, 'I will need to come with you too. Akam will need assurances that anything that is arranged is done properly, and it is best I oversee it for the safety of the group.'

It seemed unnecessary to me, but I knew that Baz was always keen to assert himself as leader of the group, so agreed to his request. I had been looking forward to getting some of my own space whilst there though, as it can become pretty intense all living together twenty-four hours a day, so I told Baz I had made arrangements to stay with a friend, and then secretly checked myself into a hotel.

I saw him the next night when we were invited to the birthday party of the guy we had spent New Year's Eve with. Unfortunately Baz got steaming drunk and began making remarks about some of the girls who were there, announcing things like, 'She is well up for me,' and pointing obviously at the subject of his comment, and so leaving the girls feeling uncomfortable. I was embarrassed by his slimy behaviour, and left soon after. I understood that he was pleased to be back in the company of females and away from the testosterone-filled base, but I did feel his behaviour was inappropriate.

At the same time, annoyingly, we were missing a mission back at base, which JP texted me about. 'We went to the front today, got eyes on Basheer, it is huge! This is not a village, it is a massive place. We are all going to fucking die!'

I had to laugh. I was like, 'Cool, when are we going?!'

Basheer is a town just three kilometres south of Kirkuk that was taken by Daesh in June 2014. It was particularly galling at the time as it was the first Shi'ite town to fall to them, and it was the Peshmerga who had been trying to hold them back. While many of the areas we had come across so far on the front line were villages and hamlets, this was a larger stronghold, and the talk on the base often focused on how much everyone would like to regain it, and how important it would be. It was good to hear that the boys had got within distance of it, as perhaps this meant a move to retake it was on the cards.

The next day we headed to the meeting with the producer, who rocked up with a present of some sweets from the UK, which was a good start. He told us that they had lined up some filming in Syria, and were planning on heading on to Iraq afterwards, and would like to visit us. Baz kept trying to assert himself as the leader during the conversation, telling the guy, 'This is my unit. If you do any filming there that we aren't happy with, I will hunt you until the end of my days.'

I laughed to try and lighten what he was saying, and

told the poor guy he was welcome to come and check it out, which he did once we were back at base. My concern was we weren't doing enough at the time to give them as much footage as they needed if he was to bring down a camera crew, but he seemed pleased enough with what he saw on his scouting mission.

The residency card that I had got on my initial arrival in Kurdistan was called a 'single entry' and lasted two months. Then after that you would get a card that had to be renewed every six months. While I had been at Dwekh, this had been no problem to get hold of. You needed a responsible person in the country who would say that you would be under their care whilst there – effectively they are a kind of guarantor. At IDET, though, it proved much harder. My latest card was due to expire at the end of January, and Sean, Ryan and Ross had not yet managed to get one since they had arrived, which was starting to bother them. The attitude from the Pesh bosses was very much that we didn't need one when we were on their base as no one was going to check our cards – a fair enough point, but it meant that we felt as though we were becoming semi-prisoners as to have one is a legal requirement. It is very hard to get out of the country without a valid card, at least without facing a hefty fine, so it was beginning to feel as though avoiding helping us with cards was a way the Pesh were ensuring we stayed and fought. I had heard of volunteers in other areas having their cards taken off them if they tried to leave, although I had looked into this, and it was possible to go back to the office and say you had lost yours and you needed a replacement. It was a hassle, but people withholding your card was illegal, so this was the best way around it. I advised a few people to do this who were beginning to feel they were being trapped in the country by other groups.

It didn't help our situation that the nearest office was in Suli, which was about a hundred and ten kilometres away, or an hour and a half drive each way, so no one was keen to spend a day going there with us to sign the forms on our behalf. Eventually though, one of the Pesh agreed, and we set off to get it sorted.

This was my first trip to Suli apart from briefly passing through after I arrived in February 2015. The city is set against a backdrop of several mountain ranges, which at this time of year were snow-capped. It made for quite an impressive sight as we drove towards it. Suli houses around one and a half million people, of various religions and backgrounds, although it is ultimately a Kurdish city. Over the years it has seen a lot less trouble and unrest than Kirkuk and I was told it is an economically important place. Walking around, the population seemed to be quite modern in its thinking, with a relaxed vibe, women and men chatting together in the street, and the fashion quite Western in appearance.

It would have been naive to think we were totally safe there though and could let our guard down. While the area was traditionally Kurdish, and had been under Kurdish rule since the city was liberated in 1991 with no attempt by Daesh to take over, like so much of the country, it had been infiltrated. Just a week or so before our visit, raids had been carried out on a Daesh terror cell within the city which had reportedly been planning attacks across Kurdistan. So while we had a bit of a wander around after getting our paperwork done, we made sure to always keep our wits about us.

Shortly after our trip to Erbil, the Lieutenant told us he was going to be away for a bit as he was heading to America. It turned out that he was actually in possession of a green card! Apparently he had spent lots of time over there before this particular war, but now he was back here, he had to make occasional trips to ensure it stayed valid or to renew it, as they last for ten years at a time. I could only assume he had been given this card in exchange for the translation duties he had carried out for the American forces during previous conflicts.

Akam had various successful businesses on the go within the Kirkuk region, which meant he probably had a better life in Kurdistan than the US on some levels, but it was still striking that when things had begun kicking off he had chosen to be in Kurdistan and fight for his country, rather than escaping to America – something the majority of the rest of the country could only dream of. I already liked the Lieutenant, but this information gave me a new-found respect for the man.

In his absence a man called Ali, who worked alongside Akam with the Pesh, was to take control of us. He was more softly spoken than Akam and radiated less of Akam's crazy energy, but was a nice guy, and also spoke English with an American accent.

One day though, Baz got a call from Akam, who told him that he had got a security job for us Westerners in Suli and we were all to head there. Baz called us all into a room and explained: 'He wants us to go there indefinitely for this security job, which will pay $300 a month, and will see us in a huge house with new clothes, a suit each, food and really good treatment.'

'What is the security job?' JP asked.

'No idea I'm afraid, mate,' replied Baz, 'he didn't give me those details, just said he had sorted it for us, he thought we should be pleased, and that is all I know.'

It was clear the room was instantly divided. There were those who were really short of money to whom this appealed, and then there were those of us – me included – who had no desire to do it at all and didn't see it as having anything to do with why we'd gone out there.

Before arguments escalated as to whether we should go or not, I suggested, 'Everyone go away for a couple of hours and think about it, then we can all say if we want to go or not, and if necessary we can split up.'

I didn't need the time to think about it – there was no way I was going. I hadn't come out here to do a paid security job that I knew nothing about for someone else.

Besides, if I had wanted that kind of role, I would have expected a lot more than $300 a month for it!

When we reconvened, Ryan, Sean, Kidd, Ash and Chris said that they were all keen to go. None of them were entirely sure what they were heading to, but as Sean pointed out, 'It's quiet here at the minute, so I am happy to go and check it out, and we can come back if it's not all that.'

That left JP, Baz, Ross and me, who all felt that staying put was the right thing to do. We knew there was a mission planned for the next day, and we were keen to be involved in that.

We later found out Ali was unhappy at what was happening – he was obviously keen that we stay and fight alongside his men while he was in charge of us, and didn't like that we were getting orders from someone currently out of the country.

Around this time a new 81mm mortar had been given to us to familiarize ourselves with, and use as necessary. Well, I say new – it was a Turkish system that was older than me, and no one had ever seen a type like it before. Again it was a sign that the Pesh didn't have the finances or the access to large supplies of top-of-the-range new weapons, but everyone did well at making do with what there was. Even Ash, who was our official mortar man as he had done lots of work with them in his previous military career, said he had never seen a system like this. He gave it the once-over anyhow to make sure there were no missing parts, and determined that it was in good working order, and we were good to go with it.

Realizing that he was no longer going to be around on the next few missions as he would be in Suli, and with one scheduled for the next day, I thought the best thing would be for me to make sure I understood it too. Time for those trusty YouTube videos and that helpful hobby of Googling . . . I spent the evening getting to grips with the mortar, which was in three parts – barrel, baseplate and bipod with sights carried separately and assembled at the front line. Mortars come in three sizes, 60mm, 81mm and 120mm, so this was the mid-size.

With 60mm mortars we had used previously, you would take the mortar shell out of the packaging and add charges to the bottom of it. These are soft gel-like C-shaped clips that go onto the thin bit of the shell, below the bulbous section, and above the fins. They go on one from the left, then one from the right so they are overlapping, and keep the shell balanced, so it keeps its trajectory. Depending on how far you want it to travel, you vary the number of charges to keep it airborne for the required time.

The 81mm however already had the clips on. They looked quite different – like squares of carpet tile with wire reinforcing mesh running through them – and you snapped off what you didn't want to use, rather than adding the clips.

Then, as before, the safety pin was removed, then a

round dropped down the tube to fire it. It was quite a different method, but I felt that I understood the weapon by the end of the evening, and would be capable of holding my own on the front the next day if we got the chance to use it.

The next morning we said our goodbyes to the five who would be travelling on to Suli that day, and headed out with the Pesh, under Ali's command. We were told to take the Humvee, and for once, I was to drive. It was one of very few times I took on the driving role on a mission, and the first time I had driven a Humvee. This particular vehicle had been through the wars, and climbing in I struggled to see through the windscreen. The cracks crossing the glass were so bad they looked like spiders' webs and it was hard to make out the terrain ahead, while the wing mirrors appeared to be holding on by a thread. Nevertheless, I couldn't wait to get going.

Baz jumped up next to me in what is known as 'the commander's seat' – with Kidd gone to Suli, he was now officially the sole guy in charge of our group, and very keen to remind us of this. Although to be fair, given that we were all under the command of the Pesh Lieutenant, it didn't actually leave too much for the leader of the Westerners to do. Anyhow, Ross got into the back, and JP climbed up into the turret. This had been much improved from the original basic one that was supplied with the Humvee, and was a good solid addition that allowed us to have someone out top keeping an eye out and ready to fire if need be. Kidd had worked hard modifying the vehicles and the turret was accessible from inside the Humvee.

I turned the ignition, more than ready to get going, but the engine didn't want to kick in, and we had to be started with the help of jump leads. Eventually we were off. We were the rear guard, meaning we were at the back of the line, following the rest of the Pesh, and keeping an eye out behind. Not that JP always had the time to do that – the windscreen was so bad that he was having to instruct me which way to drive half the time! Yet more poor equipment, despite it belonging to the country's official army. The poor guys really did need more funding.

After about half an hour we pulled up at a forward operating base set back from an area of the front line that I hadn't visited before. The aim from here was to get eyes on Basheer, which we were instantly able to do. Basheer is a big town as opposed to a village, and JP was probably right that if Daesh had decided to attack us at that point we would have been easily outnumbered and probably died. We were parked up in the cul-de-sac area next to the building and waited. Instructions were just to stay put for a while, so we sat chatting, then Baz began complaining that he didn't feel well. His glands and throat were swollen and he felt out of sorts generally. Not good when your medic is wanting to call in sick! At midday the chow wagon rocked up to dole out the lunch, and turning to us Baz asked: 'You don't mind if I hitch a ride back with the wagon, do you? I feel rough as, and not much is happening, so I am sure you will be fine without me.'

We nodded, and he headed off, leaving us to sit quietly, waiting for something to happen. Then Ali decided he was going to take a group to the front line, which was about seven minutes' drive in front of us. We watched him pass over us and fill his team with lots of Pesh who had just arrived and had no experience under their belt.

'Great,' JP muttered, 'he's taking the fucking Ant Hill Mob with him.'

It was a bit of banter, but at the same time we did feel genuinely pissed off that he was leaving us and the rest of the Pesh at the FOB, preferring these new people. They spread themselves at intervals along the berm, and we watched as Ali organized them while keeping an eye on everything.

We decided we might as well keep busy by getting out the new mortar and setting it up, to see how it all fitted together and for practice. But around 15:00, just as we had got it all up and looking good, it all kicked off up ahead. We could see mortars landing in around the guys and dust flying up, while shots whistled over their heads.

JP grabbed the radio. 'Ali! Do you need us at the front? We can bring the 81mm mortar and get stuck in.'

'Stay put for now, but thanks,' came the reply.

We were as frustrated as could be that we couldn't get up to join them, but in the hope that the fire might get heavier and we would get a call, we decided to get ourselves ready to go the second that happened. We packed the mortar back down, crammed everything into whatever space we could find in the Humvee, then sat and waited. Suddenly Ali was on the radio: 'Get up here now, boys!'

We didn't need a word more encouragement, and before he had even cut comms, I had accelerated hard in the direction of the front line. The dust added to my lack of ability to see through the windows, and JP yelled down from the turret instructions such as 'Hard left!' 'Straight, but there's a lot of rocks to get over!' to get us there as quickly as possible in one piece.

There was a steep slope leading up to the front line and we stopped on that, just short of the top, and jumping out grabbed the mortar.

A member of NATO Special Forces approached us. 'Bring that along here,' he instructed, motioning to a point he wanted us to set it up. We quickly pieced it together, as I silently thanked the time I had put into learning about it the night before. If he couldn't tell that I had been a civilian before coming out to Iraq, then I would be happy.

Just as JP pulled out the shell to load into the top of the mortar the SF guy stopped him. 'You have fired this mortar before, right?'

'It's not even been tested,' JP replied. 'We only got it a few days ago, but our mortar guy gave it a once-over and said it was good to go.'

The SF guy – who said he had never even seen this old mortar system either – stood back. 'There's no fucking way I'm dropping the first one!'

At that Ross did a smart U-turn, mumbling, 'I better go

and erm, get a erm multitool from the Humvee.' JP, shell in hand, looked at me imploringly.

'Not me, mate,' I told him, tapping my chest with my fist, 'I'm just a civilian.' Yes, I was outrageous enough to pull that trump card when it suited me . . .

Backing away to take cover behind the vehicle I watched as JP swore to himself, and took a deep breath before lifting the shell. Just as his arms went up, there was a loud dull thump as a mortar landed about thirty metres away – just out of range of causing us any damage, but close enough that everyone's thoughts were that the next was likely to be on target.

'We need to get out of here, man!' shouted Ali, dashing down from his lookout spec, about fifteen metres over to our left, motioning to us and the rest of his men. 'This is getting too much, take cover and get back to the FOB!'

The Pesh all ran for their vehicles, and keeping low, Ross and I ran to help JP take the mortar apart. I was keen to stay and fight, but Ali's reaction did match with how hairy things were getting, and we needed to do as instructed. After loading the equipment, we all piled in. I turned the switch, but nothing happened. As the sound of mortar fire continued around us, I swore, and tried again and again, but there wasn't the slightest stutter from the engine, or even a click to tell me I was on the right track. It was well and truly dead – the troubles starting it first thing that morning clearly hadn't been a one-off.

By then the rest of our guys were well out of sight, a

trail of dust all that remained to show the direction in which they had fled.

'For fuck's sake!' yelled JP, grabbing the radio and calling through to Ali. 'We need someone back here NOW to jumpstart us. We are stuck in the middle of heavy incoming.'

'Er yes, sure,' came the hesitant reply. 'I'll have someone with you right away.'

A Humvee needs to be jumpstarted by another Humvee, as it requires specific leads to link a particular connection under the passenger seat of each vehicle. It isn't jumpstarted under the bonnet like other vehicles and the power needed by a Humvee would drain most other cars anyhow. So basically there was nothing we could do without someone else and their vehicle to help us.

I tried turning the key a few more times, and looked on helplessly as another mortar fell what sounded like fifteen metres to the left of us. I was beginning to think the awful vehicle windows were a blessing in preventing us seeing just how close we could be to death. Quickly we ran through our options – we could make a dash for it, but that would leave us even more exposed. Adrenalin pumping, we discussed whether we would be just as well getting back out and finishing off what we had started with the mortar. JP in particular was keen on this, having been milliseconds from firing it when Ali shouted his orders and itching to complete. But then if we stayed put, at least here our vehicle was just over the slope, and so out of the eye line of Daesh who would hopefully think we had all retreated, and ultimately we knew this is what Ali would order us to do if he was here. None of the options we were spitting out were ideal, and as we glanced quickly around for any other escape route, we were all fully aware that it was luck more than anything that would determine if incoming fire was about to take us out.

Suddenly the charged atmosphere of the vehicle changed.

'If you're going to San Francisco . . .' The dulcet tones of JP filtered down to Ross and me from the turret.

Ross looked at me, eyes wide in horror. 'Has he lost it?'

After a moment's pause, I started laughing, and joined in. 'Be sure to wear, those flowers in your hair.'

Just a couple of days before, we had watched *The Rock*, a film set on the island of Alcatraz, and starring Sean Connery. His character is eccentric but skilled, and while trying to plot his escape from the FBI, he starts singing that song in the shower. It seemed the perfect time for us to tap into that mindset!

'You Brits are fucking insane,' muttered Ross, settling back. 'We are under attack like sitting ducks, and you think it is time for a campfire singing session?'

I shrugged, and grinning sang at him: 'If you're going to San Francisco . . .' He wasn't having it and wouldn't join in, but there was literally nothing we could do, so singing was as good as anything as far as I was concerned.

After fifteen minutes, with the assault beginning to die down a bit, but still no sign of any support from the Pesh, who we knew from our earlier drive from the FOB were stationed only seven minutes away, JP got on the radio again.

'I am going to try and get someone there, but there are still a lot of mortars coming in around you, so it is pretty dangerous. Is there no other way you can get the car started?' asked Ali.

Leaning across I grabbed the radio: 'No, Ali, I left my fucking RAC card at home today, so I am afraid there is no one on their way – it is down to you guys to get us!'

I couldn't believe we had travelled out to Kurdistan to help these guys in their fight, but they were happy to leave us stranded like this when it came down to it. It seemed life was cheap when it came to us at that moment, but not to the guys who couldn't be persuaded to come and help us!

Ten minutes later a very hesitant Pesh truck pulled up and climbing out, the soldier jumpstarted us with leads from his Humvee to ours. It worked instantly, and we both drove hell for leather back to the FOB. We were very relieved to be out of the firing line, but sad that our sing-song was over. The day hadn't finished however, as we were told we were to spend the night in our vehicles at the FOB as the Special Forces still had work to do, and we were to remain as their backup.

Parking up in the cul-de-sac we munched on dinner from the latest chow wagon visit, and tried to settle ourselves. We all had a blanket each, but as soon as it got dark the temperature plummeted. As I struggled to get comfortable, I turned to see JP all spread out and relaxed, with his own blanket as well as the one Baz had left behind. Trust him to have found it and be making himself at home.

Finally I dozed off, and woke up freezing, with numb feet, glad I had at least made it through the night – only to look at my watch and see it was only 22:30, half an hour after I had last checked. I climbed out of the Humvee and walked around to try and get warm, but the clear skies that are an almost nightly occurrence in Iraq meant it was so cold my teeth were chattering and I had to climb back in the vehicle. I turned the engine on to get the heaters going, and was dozing off again when I was woken by Ross shaking me. This time I'd moved my foot onto the accelerator and was revving the engine so loudly that Daesh probably heard in the next village. I'd just got back to sleep again when JP's yelps jerked me awake – he had rolled onto a pack of mini water bottles on the back seat, and they had burst, soaking him. We eventually gave up on sleep, as it clearly wasn't meant to be.

At first light under Ali's instructions we headed back to the front line, but there was no sign of movement from Daesh and the Special Forces had finished their reconnaissance, so we returned to base.

In the lead-up to this mission Ross hadn't made much of an impact on me. He was a nice guy, but was constantly worried about getting things wrong. In retrospect I think it was hard for him as he was the newest guy on the team, and we had all fallen into our own rhythms and way of life, and he was trying to do his best to fit in with us. But on the mission he had been helpful and held his own, and I began warming to him and decided I would do what I could to encourage him. Sadly it wasn't to be as Baz pulled him to one side, and told him: 'Ross, you aren't fitting into the group, and I don't think you belong here. You are like a fish out of water. It would be better for us all if you left.'

I didn't think it was fair on the poor guy, and given time I think Ross could have added plenty to the group, but he didn't put up much of an argument, instead packing his kit and heading back to the States. At moments like that it felt that Baz was being too controlling.

'It is like he is creating Baz's gang,' I said to JP, 'as opposed to thinking what is best for the team.'

14

MISSION ACCOMPLISHED?

As always seems to be the case in Kurdistan, the paper-work for our residency cards on our visit to Suli had not been simple, and we were told we had to go back to the office again to get it sorted. Baz and I were told by the Pesh to just give them our passports and they would do it for us. Not a chance. As Baz told them, 'Where my passport goes, I go.' It wasn't that we didn't trust them, but if anything happened to our passports we would be well and truly stranded, so neither of us was willing to let that happen.

The guy in charge replied, 'Listen, you have to play the game here a bit or you have to go.'

'Well I'll go home, then,' I replied. 'You are not taking my passport off me.' And they backed down.

Heading back to Suli we arranged to call in on the guys and see how their security job was going – or not going, as I had gathered from WhatsApp messages with

Sean. True enough, they had been put up in a brand-new six-bedroom house just to themselves, on a secure compound, with a massive kitchen, huge TV, and access to a gym. They had also been given a couple of new bits of clothing, but that was the extent of it. No suits, pay, or work had been forthcoming. From the state of the house it looked as if the guys had done nothing but sit around and eat pizzas the whole time they had been away!

After we got the residency cards sorted we decided to explore the city a bit more, and visited the Amna Suraka Museum – or Red Prison as it is known in English. The museum is housed in an old Ba'ath intelligence headquarters and prison, and looks at the treatment of people under Saddam's regime, in particular the Kurds. The Iraqi intelligence service would bring their prisoners here and put them through the most brutal and horrific physical and mental torture.

Although I had heard plenty of stories about the treatment of Kurds under the Ba'ath Party's rule, it still came as a shock when laid out so visually in front of me, and was a truly sobering experience. Even the most hard-hearted person couldn't have failed to be moved by what some of those poor people went through, and it gave me a clearer understanding of how the recent history of the Kurdish people has shaped them.

Back at the base I was starting to get homesick for certain aspects of British life. Not that it ever took much to cheer me up though. On one trip to Kirkuk when we went to the supermarket to get our shopping, I came across a frozen pack of McCain's Smiles – the potato rounds that look like smiley faces. I loved those back in the UK, and the simple pleasure of finding them kept me happy for the next twenty-four hours! I have a funny photo of me in the supermarket with my McCain's Smiles – it looks like a typical scene in the UK, but for my AK lying across the top of the trolley. As I say, the vibe of Kirkuk meant we didn't feel safe, so I wouldn't even go somewhere like the supermarket without being tooled up.

During this downtime we also spent a bit of time playing with our boy's toys. I had bought a quad bike a while back with the idea that it might be of use in the field, in particular for quickly transporting anyone injured off the beaten track. Sadly it wasn't to be – I was the only one who thought that! So instead the quad remained at base for us to just have fun with. We found a good mound of earth out back that we would use as a jump, and took it in turn to do laps. It got pretty hairy at times, and there were moments when I thought I might be heading home from war with an injury inflicted in a completely unexpected way . . .

We also took an APC – armoured personnel carrier – out for a spin one day when we were bored. It was kept at the observation point on base and we'd not previously used it. The APC is not designed to actually go into battle, but is well kitted out to transport people and defend as need be. It was interesting to see inside a vehicle that until now I had only seen onscreen in war films.

It was now 8 February 2016, a year to the day since I had left the UK to join the fight, and I stopped and assessed what I had achieved. I had certainly helped to protect innocent people, killed some of the enemy, raised awareness and added financially and physically to the fight against Daesh. On a personal level I also felt I had made some incredible friends, gained a lot of new skills and learnt things about myself. But I wasn't sure it was enough. Perhaps I had had an unrealistic view of what war was like before I had gone out, but while I got a real thrill out of the days when we were at the front line actually achieving something, I had thought they would have been a much more common occurrence. I also hadn't allowed for the politics and ulterior agendas both throughout the country and in the various fighting groups that seemed to slow everything down and make it harder to make any headway.

I lay on my bed and had a very serious think about the future and what I wanted next. There was constant talk about Basheer, and how there was to be a big offensive on the town soon. This was something I was desperate to be involved in, but the talk had gone on for so long, I was seriously doubtful that it would ever happen, and didn't want to remain just to hold out for that. I know I had vowed in the beginning to stay out there until Daesh were defeated, but the person who made that promise now seemed very much idealistic and in the past. I was still keen to be involved, and if I could be of genuine help that was still my main priority, I just wasn't convinced I was helping enough that the huge sacrifices I had made to be there were worthwhile.

I had watched other people struggle about whether to stay or go, and they were often in real turmoil over it. Everyone has given up a lot to be there and has a huge belief in the cause, so it feels almost traitorous to leave. Some people hang on and on as they have no family or whatever to go back to at home, but ultimately everyone needed to be responsible for their own end date and know what is right for them. In the end I decided I wasn't quite at that stage, and would give it another couple of months with IDET, and then reassess.

Throughout early February we did various recces to different positions along the front line with Akam, who had returned from the US, but there was very little action. In fact it was so quiet that we even got to make use of a volleyball court that a few of the Pesh guys had created. It sounds insane, but they had drawn it out on a quiet day at the front, and whenever they were sitting waiting for instructions or for Daesh to make a move, they would set up a game. We joined in one day, and it was great fun. Yet another example of how you can be within range of enemy mortars, but until it is necessary to respond, can be enjoying it as downtime!

One day does stick out in my mind during this period though, for the bizarre insight it gave me into Daesh minds. We headed to part of the front line we had visited a few times before, and the Lieutenant told us to bring along the 81mm mortar and three rounds so that we could finally give it a good try on the nearby Daesh-occupied village. I was happy that we were finally going to get to fire it! We got the parts out and put it together. A Special Forces guy was with us again and took charge, so we all stood back and held our breaths. He lined the mortar up, dropped the shell into the mortar tube . . . and nothing happened.

He removed the shell and put it to one side while he carried out his inspection – not that it stayed there for long. A nearby Pesh soldier who had the same mortar scurried over and grabbed it for use in his! Soon enough the SF guy discovered that there was no firing pin in the mortar. I messaged Ash about it, as he had inspected it previously, and he swore blind that it had been there before, and the only thing we could conclude was that one of the Pesh had 'borrowed' it for their own weapon and either not mentioned it, or lost it. Sticky may still have been based back at Dwekh, but there were definitely several of the lads here who could have given him a run for his money.

After that not too much happened for a few hours, although some of the Special Forces guys were there and sent out a drone to try and get some more intel on a nearby Daesh village. We had been told that Daesh had their own homemade drones, but so far had seen no sign of them. I had laughed when someone had explained to me how they did it.

'They hang a camera from the bottom of a balloon, then attach it to the end of a really long piece of fishing wire and let it float off. They control how far it goes with the line, and when it reaches the required distance, Daesh try and get their version of intel. Then they reel it back in when they are finished. Of course if the wind is blowing in the wrong direction, they have no chance!'

I'd never heard anything so ridiculous in my life! People were forever claiming that Daesh were rich – depending on who's talking, the theory can be thanks to oil, secret funding from other Arab states, fanatical billionaires or many other sources – so surely they could have got their hands on some proper drones?

Anyhow, shortly after we had watched the allied drone head on its way, a splodge appeared in the air above the Daesh village, and slowly began making its way in our direction. As it got closer it looked to be something round with something smaller hanging beneath it.

'They are sending a drone as well! Shoot that mother-fucker down!' Akam instructed.

Instantly everyone, me included, was firing off shots, but it was Crazy Pesh who took centre stage. Jumping onto one of the trucks, he grabbed a Dushka and let rip. He was shouting and leaping around while firing, but suddenly he lost his balance and fell off the truck. It was typical of him to be going for it 100 per cent, but become so carried away. As the drone got closer it turned slowly from floating sideways to face us, and it became clear that yes it was a balloon – but not any old balloon. We all strained to see, as it looked like it had a face of some sort on it.

After it dropped to earth, some Pesh instantly ran over but I was more cautious – if this had come from Daesh, who was to say what it was. It might contain ricin or anything.

But they began grinning and held it up – the face belonged to Dora the Explorer! We all fell about laughing at the cute kid's cartoon image. What a choice. There was a piece of string hanging from the bottom, but no camera to be seen, although that was what we had to assume had been attached originally. We all got photos holding on to our new prized souvenir of war, without realizing just how much attention it would get. It was one of IDET's most retweeted photographs, and was picked up by various news sources. I am sure Nickelodeon were anything but impressed at one of their star characters being linked to Daesh, but anything that helps to poke fun at the enemy is fine by me!

Meantime the boys had now spent a few weeks in Suli waiting on this security job that just didn't seem to be forthcoming. They were bored and from the tone of the messages, losing the will to live. They still didn't even know what the job actually was – one story was that it was to guard an oil pipeline that ran through a village where the locals were tapping into it and nicking the oil, another was that it was some high-up official who needed personal security. But either way it became clear the contract had fallen through and the boys decided to head back to base and join us. Akam never really gave them a good explanation as to what had gone wrong or apologized for wasting their time. In Kurdistan something like this was not seen as a big deal.

The one person who didn't return from Suli was Sean. His WhatsApp messages had expressed his increased irritation with the situation. As he told me, 'We are getting so few chances to make a difference. I feel like I am wasting my life. Fuck this, I have a family back home and I'd rather be with them.' So after having given it a go for six weeks, he jumped on a plane from Suli and headed back to the States. I was sorry to see him go, but completely understood his thinking, and I wasn't surprised as I had seen it was on the cards.

A few days later it was Valentine's Day. I got some lovely messages of support from people who have got behind what I am doing who knew we would be out there alone and wanted to cheer us up. Some of the lads joked that we were amassing our own fan club, and while I don't actually know these people that is too bizarre an idea for me! Baz didn't seem to mind it, though, in fact JP and I had commented on more than one occasion that he was becoming far too involved with female supporters. He seemed to be developing all sorts of bizarre relationships with these girls, even when he hadn't met them, and one day would be talking about 'the love of my life', then the next would be on the phone shouting the most horrific abuse at them. Everyone in the room would end up uncomfortable about it all, and I was sort of glad for these girls that he was in a different country to them.

Later in the afternoon JP and I were out back messing about on the quad bike when Baz came out and said: 'Time to go, there's something on the cards from some intel.'

It clearly wasn't urgent as although we were ready within minutes, we had the usual long wait for the Pesh to organize themselves. At times like this I felt like we were the least QRF people in the world.

We drove to the front, this time in the MRAP with Kidd driving, Baz in the front with him and the rest of us in the back. We headed to the same area where we had got stranded in the Humvee – but although we waited for an hour, there was nothing happening. So we were instructed to pull back to the FOB, and again parked up in the cul-de-sac for another freezing cold night. Baz made the announcement that he was going to head back to base as there were a couple of new recruits arriving the next morning – perhaps he was genuinely being caring about them, or more likely I think he was just laming out, and wanted to avoid a night of no sleep and numb toes! Akam also went with him, saying he had business to attend to, and leaving a different guy in charge who I had seen around, but didn't know.

The next morning we were told to go to the front, and I drove up with several others in the vehicle, including Chris who was in the turret, and took charge of the Egyptian. By then it was beginning to become a bit of a joke to me. It had only come with a hundred and fifty rounds, in two belts of seventy-five.

Ammunition belts tend to come in one of two ways, with disintegrating or non-disintegrating links. Most Western, NATO weapons tend to use the first. The belt looks like woven material, and as the bullets feed into the weapon the links fall away and the belt disintegrates. In non-disintegrating ones, used in much of the East, particularly Russia and China, the belt is made of metal with lots of holes for the rounds, and as they go into the weapon the empty belt comes out the other side. The idea is you can refill and reuse it. The Egyptian was of this type.

So these two belts contained all the ammunition I had for the Egyptian, and put simply, that was pretty useless. I could have fired them all off in under a minute, so was seriously questioning the need to be lugging it around. In reality it felt that it was more for show than practical use. Anyhow, we went over plenty of sharp bumps on the way, and Chris passed the Egyptian into the vehicle for safety. I am not sure what was the cause, but when I picked up the weapon at the other end, I discovered it was fucked, with one of the wooden stocks practically hanging on by a thread.

But now was not the time to think about it, as JP opened the back door, saying, 'Careful and keep your heads down, looks like there are a few rounds incoming already.' As he finished his sentence sniper fire whizzed directly over our vehicle and we all instinctively ducked. Time for action. Excellent! Running low in behind the berm we looked around for the boss, awaiting our instructions.

'Just stay low for now,' he said, moving down the line. There was a Special Forces guy on our side setting up a sniper position and trying to find the source of the incoming fire.

JP waved our new boss back. 'If we set up further down the line and start shooting, drawing the fire to us, it will help the sniper on our side pick him out,' he suggested.

'No, just stay in low here,' he replied.

'But surely that is our best chance of rooting the guy out?' JP insisted.

'No,' the boss replied firmly. 'Enjoy being here without having to do anything, and letting the rounds pass over your heads.'

We all looked at each other in disbelief, and I could see every bit of JP was having to bite his tongue to stop himself going off at this man who had been put in charge of all of us.

'Besides,' added the boss, seeing our faces, 'rounds are too expensive to waste at the moment. We need to conserve them.'

'If killing the enemy is a waste of rounds, then what the fuck are we actually doing here? It's a total joke,' I muttered angrily.

I was aware that the price of weapons and ammunition had long been an issue, and that a shortage meant we had to be careful. But surely right now, with Daesh firing on us and JP offering up a solution to root out the shooter, it was the time to use some of that ammo? Otherwise what I had said was 100 per cent a legitimate question – why exactly why were we there? Not just at the front line that day, but why were we in the country to help at all, when we were yet again being stopped from doing so?

I sat back fuming. This same question had reared its head far too many times as far as I was concerned.

Meantime Kidd had by now seen the state of the Egyptian and was furious about it. He began saying how rare these weapons were and how it was one of the Sheikh's favourite from his collection. I was already seething at the situation we were in, and was not in the mood for over-sentimentality about weapons.

'Mate, if there really are only three hundred of this type of machine gun in the world, maybe it should be in a museum, or we could give it back to the Sheikh and buy something of our own of more use, because let's face it, it has achieved fuck all for us. Anyhow, find me a couple of nails and some glue, and it'll be right as rain in no time.'

All in all I was in a properly bad mood by the time we got back to base around 10:00 and as it turned out, this day was a tipping point for me. While I had wanted to give things a bit longer to see if they improved, the frustration that morning at being unable to do anything when the enemy was right there was too much. I was furious at the situation and felt ready to boil over, so before things went wrong, I decided enough was enough, my time in Kurdistan was up.

I went to find Baz. 'Mate, I am out of here. I have done my time, but this bullshit is getting to be too much. Sort me out a lift to the garage, I'm gonna grab a taxi back to Erbil right now.'

He tried to change my mind, but as always when I have settled on something, there is no going back.

'We are going to be going for Basheer soon, surely you don't want to miss that?' he asked.

But I had heard it all before, and much as I wanted to believe like Baz that that was the truth, I no longer could. However, I did agree to leave all my weapons and my kit behind just to keep the door open in case things showed any signs of changing significantly. Besides, what use were any of my weapons going to be to me back in the UK – even if I could get them through customs, which we all know I couldn't.

Anyhow Baz already had another problem on his hands – the two volunteers he had been waiting on had arrived, but the Sheikh had sent over a third, who was completely unknown to us and hadn't been vetted, something we had put a lot of effort into doing.

I went for a final walk with JP and the dogs and we had a long chat about our experiences and the future. I said to him, 'Mate, I know you are desperate for a scrap, but I don't think there is a scrap here. At some point you have to let it go. There is nothing we haven't tried to do to help. I know everyone keeps mentioning Basheer but one day it seems we will be involved, and then the next we are cut out. Maybe it will all be left with the Ant Hill Mob to deal with! I know your heart is in the right place, but don't drag out your time here for the sake of dragging it out.'

He nodded and conceded, 'I need to give it a bit longer, but I don't think I will be far behind you, mate.'

I was absolutely gutted to be leaving him. We have been shot at, mortared at, moaned and laughed together, and I have learned so much from him, and hopefully been able to teach him a thing or two as well. There is no question that we will be friends for life.

I didn't tell the Pesh I was leaving, although Baz told Akam but he didn't come and say goodbye so I guess he wasn't happy about my departure. All the Westerners saw me off though. The experiences I had had with them had created a bond that you just didn't get in 'normal' life, so I was genuinely really sad to be saying goodbye to them. I knew I would stay friends with most of the lads.

Back in Erbil I checked into my usual hotel, which was a nice place with a gym, a pool and decent food, and spent a few days in my own company, gathering my thoughts. In the army I know they sometimes take soldiers to a kind of halfway house in another country to get their heads back in order before returning to the UK. Erbil was like that for

FIGHTING ISIS

me. I tried to gather some ideas for my future. Was it possible that I could find a different way to help the Kurds be
rid of Daesh once and for all? Was there anything in the
UK for me to go back to, and was I happy to practically
be starting again financially, with no house or job, and
friends and family having drifted?

I had a couple of meetings with other groups who put
forward ideas while I was in Erbil, and Googled options
back in the UK, but my head wasn't really ready to decide
yet.

Then it was time to go home. I flew from Erbil International Airport to Istanbul Airport Ataturk, where I had
to wait on a connecting flight. I went through security and
was sitting by the departure gate waiting for it to open
when a British guy came in with a big pair of Beats head-
phones and put them down, mumbling something to me
about hating the airport. He sat down and started chatting about how he had been flying through from Erbil.

'Yeah, I saw you on the last flight,' I said.

We were talking about the state of Kurdistan and generally passing the time when another random British guy,
around twenty-eight years old, walked over, making a
direct beeline for me. 'Sorry to interrupt, this might sound
stupid, but are you Tim Locks?'

I nodded.

'It is fantastic to meet you! I saw you before but wasn't
sure it was you. I am an avid follower of you and what
you have been doing in Kurdistan. My mates are over
there, I can't wait to tell them.'

He shook my hand, and said, 'Assuming you are on this flight to Heathrow, I'd like to buy you lunch or a beer at the other end?'

It was really humbling and I felt embarrassed, but said, 'I really appreciate that and don't think I am brushing you off, but I have to get straight on with stuff.' What I really meant was, 'I imagine I will be stopped for several hours for questioning,' but I didn't want to say that.

I watched him head back to his mates and point me out, and the guy sat next to me looked at me and said: 'Am I some sort of dick? Are you famous, and I am just sitting here chatting to you about how hot Istanbul Airport is?!'

'Not at all, mate.' Then there was an awkward silence so I told him what I had been up to, although I felt self-conscious about the attention and compliments it elicited. It has always been a tricky aspect of what I was doing. I wanted to draw everyone's attention to the horrors of Daesh, and everything that is going on in Kurdistan and the surrounding areas, but I was always aware of not wanting to sound like I had gone out there like some saviour. I felt like I hadn't achieved as much as I wanted, and too much praise was embarrassing. I was also worried at the other end of the scale that people might judge me for not having done enough.

Landing in the UK I avoided going through the IRIS queue – I always have this deep-rooted fear of getting locked in one of those boxes with sirens going off and flashing arrows pointing at me: 'Question this man!'

Instead as usual I was pulled aside quietly at passport control for my questioning with Special Branch. It went on longer than ever, and all laptops and phones were handed over for inspection.

One of the first things I did once I got out of the airport was go for a huge slap-up meal. No red, green or yellow shit with rice in sight. Then what did I do? I took a photo of it, as well as my next few meals, and sent them to all the boys back in Kirkuk. Mean perhaps, but I couldn't resist. A lamb roast with Yorkshire pudding, veg and lashings of gravy, Chinese take-out, a pulled-pork burger with nachos . . . I just couldn't get enough of the food back home. Needless to say my photos went down badly, particularly with JP, who threatened to defriend me! But it was all about life's simple pleasures.

One night I slept through a bunch of frantic calls from JP, and when I eventually spoke to him he had some horrific news. A newspaper had written a piece on Baz's efforts in Iraq, and off the back of that it seemed they had been contacted by the police. Baz was not the good man he had attempted to portray himself to be, but instead was a convicted rapist wanted by the courts back in the UK. I listened in shocked silence as JP told me: 'I'm looking at the article now, mate. In July 2015 he was convicted of two counts of rape, one of common assault, and had already pleaded guilty to ABH and assault by beating. He went on the run before the sentencing, so basically was out here just to escape that. He got seven years.'

JP said that Baz must have got a heads-up the article

was coming out, as he had left the base the night before, and no one knew where he had gone, but added: 'I don't know what he is going to do now. No group will have him. If he survives Daesh, I'm not sure he will survive any Westerners who come across him.'

'Fucking hell!' I swore, thinking back on his worrying behaviour with women, and wishing I had known then what I knew now, when I'd have had a chance to show him what I thought of rapists. To think I had spent time with this disgusting excuse for a person made me sick.

When I first went out to Kurdistan I assumed all the Western volunteers were motivated by the same simple thought I had. 'Right, I need to help the Kurds, how can I do that? Ah yes, go out and fight.' It only gradually became clear that for some of the others out there helping the Kurds came second. They were there to avoid the law, to escape a miserable home life to find fame and fortune, to prove themselves or to carry on living the military life they loved. After they had decided they needed to do that and looked around to work out how, only then did they settle on Kurdistan. Realizing that was a bit of an eye-opener for me but at the same time I was lucky to meet up with so many people whose hearts were in the right place.

I was pleased to hear that Baz was caught by the British police in the end, but in the meantime it was a case of planning my own future. I had no home, no car, a seriously reduced amount of savings, and no definite career plans. It wasn't the nicest situation to be in. But one thing I hadn't counted on was the generosity of others. Several incredible people got in touch with me directly, and also through a friend of mine to surprise me, and did what they could to make my transition to life back here as easy as possible.

As one person told my friend: 'I can't go out there to fight alongside the Kurds, so I want to help someone who has. What Tim has done is a selfless act, so it is time someone did some selfless acts for him.'

Another guy, when I questioned why he would help me, retorted: 'You think you are the only good person on this planet?'

It was all exceptionally humbling, and gave me hope that there were plenty of Brits who were aware of what was happening in the Middle East, and felt strongly about it too. I wasn't sure I felt right about accepting the offers of help though, until my friend pointed out, 'You have done your bit, mate, let others do theirs, even if it is in a different way to going out there and actually fighting the fight.'

So I accepted with fervent thank yous.

This time back in the UK I felt differently to my trip in summer 2015, when I was frustrated to be here, and felt like an outsider. This time I felt that it was right place for me.

I have thought a lot about my time in Kurdistan since coming home, and the reality is I think we came to the party too late as far as the war is concerned. By 'we' I mean all of the volunteers. The real fighting where they needed our help was done in the first half of 2014 – that was the time when we could have made a difference. A lot of the volunteers could see this, and recognized it for the convoluted drawn-out stalemate it had become. But everyone was petrified of leaving in case that monumental life-changing fight that they wanted to be involved in was around the corner. The time, the money, the emotional commitment were huge and people didn't want to go home after making big sacrifices only to miss the chance of defeating Daesh. I know I thought that.

For now I am throwing myself into life back here. Given that the gym plays such a large part in my life, it made sense for me to set up my own PT company, Wolf-Pak, to train others. But I always have one eye on everything happening abroad. And what concerns me is that despite the fact that Daesh are slowly failing in Kurdistan, I don't think as a group they are anywhere near finished – that would be a naive way to see them. But I think the fighting is going to be done in a different way. Instead of all-out war in certain towns and countries, I envisage that sadly covert and hugely psychologically damaging attacks like Tunisia and Paris will happen again.

I will always have a place in my heart for Kurdistan, and learnt so much about people, about living in a different culture, military life and myself while I was there. I will never ever regret my decision to go, and it has become part of my history and who I am. While Western governments stand back and watch, never having the courage to deal with Daesh for fear of offending or getting drawn into further violence, it feels like it is only us volunteers who are at least trying. At the first sign that I can be of genuine use back out there, I can promise I will be at that airport before you know it.

If you would like to continue following Tim's journey, you can do this on his instagram page @tim_locks.

APPENDIX: KIT

I am forever being asked for a full kit list, either by people wanting to head out and join the fight, or just out of interest. I have changed and honed what I take over time – for example I no longer take razor blades as they are two a penny in Kurdistan, and in the beginning I didn't realize just how necessary mosquito repellent would be. There is also no guarantee on what you will be allowed through the airport, but I have had no problems with any of the below. Everyone will have their own preferences of course, so each person's list will be very specific to them, but this is how mine currently stands:

- British Army issue Osprey vest with the soft armour – Kevlar
- Four small side plates. Plates are available in Kurdistan, but there is no guarantee how good they

will be, and it is not easy getting plates any bigger than this through customs.

- Kevlar helmet
- Tan desert boots
- High-Tech Magnum boots
- Camouflage trousers and jacket. I checked with the group I was joining the type of cammo they used and based it around that.
- A selection of civvy clothes. On downtime the last thing I want to be doing is barrelling into shops looking like Rambo and drawing attention to myself.
- T-shirts
- Hoodies
- Underwear
- Flip-flops. Might sound daft, but the best thing for round the house, and gives your feet a nice break after army boots!
- Sleeping bag
- Waterproof zip-lock bags
- Handheld radios
- Night-vision goggles. The locals love these, and it is a good way to make friends with them!
- Binoculars
- GPS
- Camelbak. The water comes in such tiny plastic bottles in Kurdistan, I found this was the only useful and compact way to carry a good supply of fluids.
- Holster
- Slings

- Protein drinks
- Energy bars
- Water purification tablets – the water out there is undrinkable without.
- Knee pads. These are crucial if you don't want to be in agony after endless hours kneeling / lying / crawling across the ground at the front line.
- Gloves, as it gets bitterly cold in winter.
- Hats and scarves, for warmth when it is cold, protection when it is windy and the sand is whipping round like crazy, and also useful for anyone who wants to conceal their faces in photographs.
- Torch
- Penknife, both for my own use and as presents for the locals, who love collecting good penknives.
- US dollars as these are the most easily exchanged currency in Kurdistan.
- Ballistic sunglasses
- Normal sunglasses
- Batteries
- Solar panels to charge
- Washbag
- Mosquito spray – I always say if you come with nothing else, this is my biggest necessity. The little buggers are everywhere.
- A field first-aid kit
- Any medications. While you can buy meds here for pennies, I prefer to have brands that I know and am happy with.

ACKNOWLEDGEMENTS

I think it is pretty clear from my story who I have to thank for making my time in Iraq bearable! But special mentions need to go to JP, for always having my back, and Tex, for making me laugh, even when times were tough.

Thank you to every person who messaged me, supported me, and donated to the cause. Not only did you help to keep me out there and entertain me during the downtime, but you did a good job of reminding me who and what I was fighting for.

Then to Emma Donnan, thanks for seeing the potential in my story and making the writing process painless – even, dare I say it, fun! I'm sure I've not been the easiest to work with, but I honestly couldn't have done this with anybody else.

Ingrid Connell and all the guys at Pan Macmillan, thank you for giving me a chance to tell my story, being straightforward and helpful to work with, and for understanding why this fight against Daesh is so important.

Then James Willis – BJ – thanks for getting the deal in the first place. The Nando's chicken challenge is now on . . .

Thanks to 'Maverick' and 'Horse Lady' for running my life, Susu for helping me with everything and anything, and Bill R for being a voice of reason, and helping me to see things differently. Cheers to Terry Turbo for checking up on me, and the Nando's boys for seeing me off and seeing me back.

Finally, thank you to a thoughtful, kind, and special person for listening to my stories, for taking an interest, and just for being there. You know who you are.